THE
NEW
WORKFORCE

Jan —
Live long live well!
Harvest Harlun

Thanks for attending!

Harv

THE NEW WORKFORCE

FIVE SWEEPING TRENDS THAT WILL SHAPE YOUR COMPANY'S FUTURE

HARRIET HANKIN

American Management Association

New York • Atlanta • Brussels • Chicago • Mexico City • San Francisco
Shanghai • Tokyo • Toronto • Washington, D.C.

This publication is designed to provide accurate and authoritative information in regard to the subject matter covered. It is sold with the understanding that the publisher is not engaged in rendering legal, accounting, or other professional service. If legal advice or other expert assistance is required, the services of a competent professional person should be sought.

Library of Congress Cataloging-in-Publication Data

Hankin, Harriet.
    The new workforce : five sweeping trends that will shape your company's future / Harriet Hankin.
        p.   cm.
    Includes index.
    ISBN 0-8144-0829-X
    1. Labor supply.   2. Longevity.   3. Organizational change.   4. Labor supply—Effect of technological innovations on.   I. Title.

HD5706.H363   2004
331.1—dc22

2004009793

Printing Number

10   9   8   7   6   5   4   3   2   1

To my Bobby and my Lindsay—all
I've ever needed for happiness

Contents

Acknowledgments

I always read acknowledgments. I love guessing who the people are to the author. I would never believe that I would get the opportunity to keep anyone guessing about who my people are to me.

To Melinda: who wrote and wrote and wrote and then rewrote and rewrote and rewrote—well, we finally finished. Let's celebrate again! Thanks to Carl and the girls for their support.

To Lori: she doesn't ever want to see a dictation tape again—ever! She also kept me going, researched each permission, and is completely fabulous.

To the Interns: what a group of smart people—Kate Johns, Jody Pillard, Peter Hanson, Becky Best, David Damsgaard, and Jessie Pillard—the world is lucky to have you.

To the development editor, Barry Richardson: we waited for each e-mail, are we on track or not? Praise from you caused much hooting and hollering, thank you for taking us on.

To Adrienne Hickey: our editor. Without you we wouldn't be published—you loved the concept from the start.

To Alex Johns: my business partner and friend for twenty years, thanks for every one of those years of fun and creativity—so much I've learned from you. You epitomize generosity.

Thanks to all the wonderful people I interviewed—you are each fascinating and I so enjoyed that part of the book process.

To my family and friends: Thanks for the stories. I hope I didn't get a story too mangled. I am a lucky woman to have each of you in my life.

To CGI: What a company. Thanks to all of you for putting up with the book: Gail as first editor, Kathy and the Leadership Team, and every one of you for providing such inspiration.

I have the best girlfriends: oldest, dearest—Ellen; brilliant, funny—Susan W.; dear, dear college roommate—Renee; instant best friend—Vicky; nurturing and loving—Joyce; teacher and friend—Phyllis; wise and hilarious—Natalie; beautifying my haven—Pia; compatriot and gorgeous—Molly; and my fabulous, ever present, cannot talk enough to each other—Ruthie.

My parents, my brother Art and his wife Susie and their family are always so proud of me. Both my Mom and Dad are "kveling" in heaven, keeping everyone up there bored with their boasts about their daughter's book.

I'm the luckiest Mom in the world, raising Lindsay brought out the best in me as she is truly an inspiration to those who are fortunate enough to know her. Thanks to Rob, Rick, Nancy, and Randy who gave me my practice, and I so love this family and their families.

To Bob, who walked and talked and "tugged" his way through this book. All my love for raising the children, the animals, the company, and for our beautiful life together.

THE
NEW
WORKFORCE

INTRODUCTION

As a futurist, you can be fascinating at a cocktail party. Instead of dropping names, you drop facts and figures: We are expected to live well into our 100s; the average age for young adults to marry in America is 30; the single male head of household is the fastest growing demographic group; and the University of Minnesota was able to grow an eyeball on a tadpole that eventually may help the sightless see.

This is not just science fiction; this is our future. It is also intriguing and fun. My path to the future came about quite serendipitously. In celebration of our company's 25th anniversary, we hosted an event for our clients featuring renowned futurists, Edie Weiner and Arnold Brown, as the keynote speakers. The event was a rousing success, but beyond that, I found that the "future" bug had bitten me. I have been in the field of human resources for thirty years—in the corporate world, as a consultant, and as a public speaker. Immediately following our event, I began to add the title "futurist" to my resume. There are two reasons why. One, it is very heady and interesting stuff. Two, it is extremely useful in business.

A futurist's job is to collect research, evaluate the findings, and spot recurring themes that indicate a trend. These trends provide thought-provoking insights that can guide businesses toward smarter decisions. As we struggle with the here and now, the most powerful tool at our disposal can be strategic thinking about the future. I have found the combination of futurist and HR professional to be particularly relevant. Over and over again, in my research and interviews as well as in daily business dealings, I keep hearing that "our people are our most important asset and will be even more so in the future." This is more than a well-worn cliché. It is becoming a basic truth: As we move to a more service- and information-based society, the success of our companies depends on the success of our people.

THE MAKING OF A TREND

It is exciting to talk about trends to large groups. Attendees are intrigued by the trends and often find them more helpful in solving their current needs than they initially expect. It is also interesting to watch reactions. In speeches I have delivered around the country in the last few years, it became apparent which trends captured people and which trends scared them. The trends described in this book were neither the most popular nor the most alarming, but rather they are those that offer the most useful insights for guiding both individuals and company decision makers toward understanding and preparing for the future workforce.

In this book we take an in-depth look at five major future trends. Each trend will be defined, will have facts to support it, and will have examples of what companies are currently doing to work with these trends; whenever a counter-trend is clear, it will be exposed. The five major trends described include:

- ❏ *Aging/Longer Life Expectancy.* Imagine a city the size of Philadelphia populated entirely by centenarians. How will our companies look with four generations working side by side?

- ❏ *More Varied Household Types.* From same sex partners to Mr. Moms, the face of the typical family is not so typical any more. Every concept in human resources—from benefits to time off—will be affected by this trend.

- ❏ *Generations.* As the first round of boomers are approaching 60 years old, their children are entering the workforce with a new set of demands and expectations. Will the generations need and want a different type of company?

- ❏ *Diversity.* Fueled by digital communications and shifting demographics, "political correctness," and enhanced learning systems, the business world will find itself in a workforce melting pot. This trend will lead to company needs that span a broader range of cultures, languages, and learning requirements than ever before.

❏ *Trust, Respect, and Ethics.* The workers of the future are seeking a new focus on higher purpose in all phases of their lives—including the workplace.

In the second half of the book, we discuss the impact of these trends on different areas in the talent/people side of business: the human resources field. The insights and suggestions in those chapters can be powerful tools for guiding companies in the future. I have spoken to a large array of seasoned practitioners who are experts in their field and who have shared their insights about the various ways the trends will affect how people and companies will operate. Thus, I will describe the anticipated impact of these trends on HR policies, recruiting and retention, employee benefits and compensation, learning (training) and development, and communications. I'll also share ideas and examples that help spur company creativity and preparedness.

READY OR NOT, HERE THEY COME

Each trend deserves careful consideration. Moreover, these trends, taken together, require an action plan so companies can be positioned to survive and thrive as the trends take hold. Each of the five trends will affect every organization. Changes related to these trends are happening every day. Viewed one at a time, these changes don't seem to influence "business as usual." However, as they gain momentum—cumulating into a trend—they become a force that cannot be ignored. Companies willing to get ahead of the curve—to learn and make decisions that position them to be ready for the future—will reap the rewards.

All of my conversations and research have reinforced the belief that successful companies in the future will treat their most important assets—their employees—not as inventory or a line item of expense, subject to cutbacks and right sizing, but as a wealth of corporate potential, worthy of care, respect, and treatment with a high degree of integrity. Without exception, this theme prevails in each of the trends and in their implications for every component of running a company, not just HR management. Companies that are most creative and understanding of the facts and the future will be those that actively create a workplace where people want to do their best work. This is true for all companies, regardless of size or industry.

Individuals who understand these trends and operate with knowledge of the future, will be more valuable to the company and move faster towards leadership.

THE METHODOLOGY

In writing this book, I combined several sources. To collect secondary research, a team of interns combed libraries and the Internet to find relevant data on each of the five trends and on projections about the future. I coupled these findings with research I have been compiling as part of my business for the past several years. I also conducted many interviews as primary research. I spoke with experts in every discipline of the people side of business, and with experts on the various trends. I spoke with well-rounded, well-respected business professionals who openly shared their wealth of life and business experiences.

In connecting the dots of the research and making projections of their impact on the various disciplines of human resources, I pulled primarily from my own life, from case studies and business experiences, from the interviews, and from secondary research sources. There are endnotes for those passages that are directly quoted or which include statistics from the secondary research. The rest of the information comes from any combination of the sources listed.

MAKING THE MOST OF THIS BOOK

Planning and preparing for the future is not a one-shot deal. Being prepared for the future is an exciting, dynamic process that should involve the best thinkers in an organization.

If you consider yourself a strategic thinker who cares about the future of your work, your company, and the world, you will find this book useful and insightful. Use this book as a thought starter, as a jumping-off point for discussion and debate.

One suggested approach is to create a "Future Think Tank" group. This group should include company executives and decision makers. The top leader must be involved in order for the exercise to be a success. Assign each chapter to one individual in the group, who will lead the discussion of that chapter. Apply each trend to your company and talk through what that trend means to your organization. Discuss the human resources impact chapters and the ideas in them. Brainstorm in the classic sense: There are no bad ideas, it is open season on everything, and no current policies or procedures are sacred. Make sure that new ideas are not dismissed out-of-hand. At the very least, this will start a discussion and bring the future one step closer. Hopefully, though, discussion will lead to putting into place strategies and plans that respect and anticipate the trends. As with any strategic exercise, debate will lead to plans and actions that will make your company ready for the future.

A couple of slogans come to mind: "The future is now" and "Knowledge is power." I would tweak those a bit. I believe that *Preparation* for the future is now" and "Knowledge *plus action* is power." My hope for this book is that it will jumpstart the preparation, share the knowledge, and spur strategic actions with measurable success.

PART 1

THE FIVE MAJOR EMERGING WORKFORCE TRENDS

In the first half of this book we'll take a look at five emerging workforce trends. Our research shows that these trends are already well underway today and that they will become increasingly important in the near future. In examining each of the trends, we will define the trend and provide evidence of the trend revealing itself. We will also give examples of how companies are dealing with the trends today. If a countertrend is developing, we will present that as well.

No doubt, the impact of these five trends has already been felt in your company. As you read through the explanations, you'll probably spot examples of each trend among your own employees. By recognizing the five trends and being alert to their impact on your organization, you'll be well on your way to successfully dealing with the new workforce.

In the second half of the book, we will give you a wide variety of practical ideas to help your company develop a group of highly motivated, loyal, and productive employees, building on the five trends.

CHAPTER 1

TREND 1: LONGEVITY

THE AGING POPULATION: LIVING BETTER AND WORKING LONGER

One day last year, my father called. He was ninety-two years old at the time and living alone in Palm Beach, Florida. Since I normally called him every afternoon about 4:00, it was alarming for him to call my office early in the day. "Hi, Dad. Are you okay?" His tone reassured me that he was well and everything was fine. I immediately took a deep breath!

He said, "I know it's a little silly, but I want to trade in my car and buy a new one."

"That's not silly," I replied. "If you would like a new car, why not? What brought this on, anyway?"

"Well, when Mom was alive she always insisted we have a red car; I never wanted a red car. She insisted we have a bench seat; I always wanted bucket seats. Plus, I would like to try one of those foreign cars." I encouraged him to go ahead and make the purchase. He said, "What if I have only a few months to live? I'm 92! How much longer do I have to drive? It seems so trivial."

I said, "I have absolutely full faith that you will enjoy driving it every day you can, so go ahead and enjoy."

That same day, he drove his red Cadillac into a Jaguar dealership, fully expecting to drive out in a new car. Apparently thinking he was just an old man window-shopping, the Jaguar salespeople paid little attention to him. Perhaps with his cane and slow walk, he didn't fit their usual buyer profile. In frustration, he finally told one of the representatives that he would not be buying a Jaguar that day, but if he looked across the street in an hour he'd see him driving out from that dealer in an Infinity. True to his word, an hour later he honked the horn and waved from the driver's seat of his new, fully paid-for Infinity.

Beyond loving this story for personal reasons, it also makes a dramatic statement about how we all need to view differently a large and significantly growing part of our population. Age is not a particularly important factor in practical decision making, and we—as individuals, as businesses, and as employers—would be wise to recognize this fact.

With all the articles, statistics, and talk about "aging boomers," you may think you've already heard all you need to know about longevity. Think again. The single most significant future trend facing our society in general—and employers in particular—is the increasing life expectancy. The ramifications of this trend will affect government programs, business and the economy, the overall culture, and individual families in unparalleled ways. In the workplace, the impact of the aging population will be both powerful and positive. Companies looking to succeed in the future will learn to harness this power and accentuate the positive benefits of employing experienced, skilled, loyal, older workers.

Staying Alive, Staying Active

I often ask an audience how many people know someone in their 90s. Typically, there is a generous show of hands—most people do know someone in their 90s. Then I ask if anyone knows someone in their 100s. There are always at least one or two hands—and the number is growing.

In the United States, centenarians are in the fastest growing age group. As shown in Figure 1-1, in 1982 only about 32,000 people living in the United States were over 100 years old. By 2000, that number grew to 81,000 centenarians. If this trend continues as expected, the number of centenarians will double each decade. This is redefining who we are and how we go about working.

Many centenarians flourish these days and more are expected to do

Figure 1-1. Population aged 100 and over.

| | Population |
| | over 100 |
Year	
1982	32,000
1990	37,000
2000	81,000
2010	106,000
2020	135,000
2030	159,000
2040	174,000
2050	265,000

U.S. Census Bureau projected number of centenarians in the United States.

so in the future. The March 10, 2001, issue of *Science News* reported that centenarians today can be put in three groups:

1. 30 percent are both mentally and physically impaired by age 100.

2. 40 percent have vision, hearing, or mobility limitations and perhaps some mental impairment, but function fairly well.

3. 30 percent have few physical or mental impairments, and most of this group still live independently.

The article also stated that in a New England study of centenarians, close to 90 percent were living independently when they were 92 years old, and 75 percent were still independent when they were 97.

One welcome result of the trend toward longevity is a long-overdue revision of life expectancies by insurance companies. As is shown in Figure 1-2, age expectancies were last revised in 1980, when they predicted that men would live to about age 74 and women would live to just over age 78. Current revisions to the mortality tables used by insurance companies reflect a reduced risk of dying at all ages. Men are now expected to live just past age 78 and women to age 82. Under the old mortality tables, the ultimate life expectancy was just over 99 years. Now, that figure has been lengthened to 120.5 years![1]

Figure 1-2. Comparison of life expectancy (1980 vs. 2003).

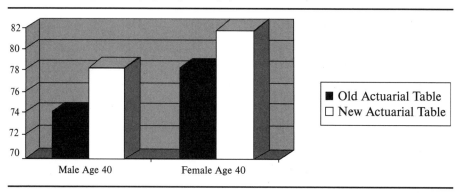

Living Longer Around the World

The longevity trend is not just an American phenomenon. This is global precedent-setting aging. Just before the turn of the century, Italy became the first country in history to have more people over the age of 60 than under the age of 20. Since then, other countries have joined the club—France, Turkey, Belgium, Spain—and more are soon to follow. Only three countries—the United States, India, and Iceland—have youth replacement populations. This means that these three countries still have enough new births each year to balance out their growing number of elders.

In the United States, our large aging population, the Baby Boomers, had families. Therefore we now have an "echo" of a large young population balancing the aging boomers, which we will discuss in Chapter 3.

Longevity in and of itself is not necessarily a good thing. What is so exciting these days is that people are not just living longer, but are also staying so much more active. Take Trevor Gamble, a retired college professor, who took up competitive sailing in his 40s, skiing and scuba diving in his 50s, and triathlons in his 60s. He would laughingly comment on his success in the triathlon, "As long as I finished, I won—there were not as many competitors in my age category!" Watch out, Trevor, that won't be true much longer.

My own husband, Robert Schoonmaker, whom you'll meet later in this book, fulfilled a life-long dream at age 70, when he bought a tugboat in Northern Canada. With no prior boating experience, he piloted his boat 1500 miles to bring it home.

Or how about this phenomenon—mall walkers by morning, people in their 60s, 70s, and 80s, are taking to the country-and-western dance floors by night. Line dancing and square dancing both are growing in popularity for the aging set.

As part of living longer and staying active, many seniors naturally will continue to work—full-time or part-time—or go back to work after "test driving" retirement. These older employees soon will start to make up a significant percentage of the overall workforce. Employers that learn to tap into this vital source of experienced workers—and, equally important, learn to accommodate whatever special considerations aging employees may require in order to continue their productivity—will be well ahead of the game in the coming years.

YOU'RE NOT GETTING OLDER, YOU'RE GETTING BETTER

In 2003, lifelong baseball professional Jack McKeon came out of retirement to manage the struggling Florida Marlins. In his more than fifty years in baseball, McKeon had never been involved in the World Series. At age 72, all he did was win the World Championship, defeating the mighty New York Yankees in the process.

My favorite prediction: By 2050, middle age will be 75–78. I feel younger already!

We all remember Bob Hope, the talented and beloved star, who died in 2003 at age 100. One of the things he was most known for was his dedication to USO shows. Mr. Hope did his final USO tour at age 87 for troops active in Operation Desert Storm. He was vibrant and hilarious to the end. However, Bob Hope is just one well-known example of the trend toward people living productive lives well into their 70s, 80s, 90s, and beyond.

Not only are we living longer, we are living better. Meet a couple of examples:

❏ *Mary Graceffa* may not be your typical 89-year-old today, but she may be in the future. As a personal banking representative at Sovereign Bank working forty hours a week, including Saturdays, she says a sincere love of helping and a desire to be around people keep her going. Mary was recently named "Woman of the Year" by the Waltham/Greater Boston Business and Professional Women's Organization. Many of Mary's coworkers see her as a role model. "More than 200 Sovereign team members have found Mary to be a respected manager, beloved coworker, surrogate mother and grandmother, a cherished friend and keeper of the peace," says Connie Fitzgerald, vice president and Metro West regional manager for Sovereign Bank. "She has shown how important it is to find a career you love and give it your all."[2]

❏ *Ida Schmidt* was the first woman graduate of the Philadelphia College of Osteopathic Medicine in 1935. Sixty-eight years later, she still actively runs her practice four days a week. Ida was named "Family Physician of the Year" by the Pennsylvania Osteopathic Family Physicians Society. Did I mention that she also still teaches one day a week?[3]

❏ Bernard Lewis, professor emeritus at Princeton University, is, in his late eighties, publishing almost a book a year. Two recent ones— *What Went Wrong? The Clash Between Islam and Modernity in the Middle East* and *The Crisis of Islam: Holy War and Unholy Terror*— made the *New York Times* bestseller lists in 2002 and 2003 respectively. The doyen of Middle East historians, he is in great demand for lectures and interviews.

❏ *Millie* is my favorite waitress at our local deli. Now in her 70s, she has been serving patrons their breakfast and lunch for forty-eight years. She's been serving us since we were teenagers! Millie still takes the bus to work every day.

There's no way to ignore it—people are living longer and staying more active. They are not becoming debilitated in their later years as often as was the case in the past. Consider a few statistics. The over-65 population increased by more than three million in the last decade, while the number of disabled people in the same group dropped by 100,000. Furthermore, the population in nursing homes is declining as is the likelihood that seniors will suffer chronic disabilities such as dementia or stroke. At the same time, the participation in the labor force of those age 65 and older has been rising over the last ten years.[4]

Accolades for the good news on the health front go not only to the medical advances and effective new drugs, but also to the seniors themselves. Better lifestyle choices—such as diet, exercise, and not smoking—are making a significant contribution as well. When I was growing up, my family was devastated the day that my grandfather had become so disabled that he was unable to live on his own, and had to move into a nursing home. He had come to this country from Russia, and had worked long and hard in his tailor shop to ensure that his son, my father, lived the American dream and could receive an excellent education. My dad worked and contributed to society well into his late 80s. I have already told you a story of my dad's vibrant independence in his 90s. He died at the age of 92, and never lived in a nursing home.

In the future, people like my dad will be the rule rather than the exception. As Figure 1-3 shows, not only will we have a population that is increasing in age, but also a population that is increasingly able to contribute to society and participate in useful life activities.

Men Are Going to the Doctor—Thanks, Viagra

One reason that men don't live as long as women is that, traditionally, most men would go to a doctor only for an emergency or when a loved one made them go. Ironically, however, the development of anti-impotence drugs, such as Viagra, has changed things. Men are now visiting the doctor in record numbers to get a prescription for the popular drug. While they are there, they are likely to get a physical check-up, leading to the discovery of other diseases and disorders such as diabetes or high blood pressure, which can then be treated proactively. This could help close the gap between male and female longevity, giving us more workers of both genders in the future.

In reviewing how longevity will affect the workforce of the future, it is important to consider not only the medical and mental health of the aging

Figure 1-3. Comparison of percentage of elderly disabled (1982-1999).

Year	Disabled Elderly	Percent of Total Elderly
1982	7.1 Million	26.9
1994	7.5 Million	22.5
1999	7.0 Million	19.7

population, but its financial health as well. The financial health of this population is important to employers because it will determine how early people will retire. At the same time, it will guide, as workers get older, whether workers *have* to work to survive or *choose* to work to fulfill their desires. Many even go to work to just keep busy and stay active. With the changing economy, the financial picture for the older worker is a moving target. We do know that living longer coupled with the American crisis of inadequate savings (which we'll discuss in Chapter 8) will make available to companies a talent pool that increasingly includes the more mature worker.

OLDER AMERICANS ARE WORKING

Not only are we living longer and living better, we are staying more active and wanting to work. According to AARP, by 2025, workers age 55 and older will be more than 20 percent of the total workers—that's more than one in five workers.

Among the reasons why the size of this portion of the labor force is growing are:

❑ The sheer volume of baby boomers

❑ Health improvements

❑ Occupations that are less physically taxing

❑ Financial considerations—people simply can't afford to retire

❑ A growing interest in making a meaningful contribution through work[5]

Despite the long-time perception that older workers are less flexible, research is showing that the opposite is true. Part-time work is a growing trend among workers of all ages, as dual income families are opting for less money in exchange for more time to care for their families. Specifically, though, part-time work is also increasingly popular with the older worker and is much more common among older women than older men. A particularly interesting trend is that part-time work as a transition to retirement is increasingly common.

I know of several women who love fashion and at a "mature" age work as sales staff at their favorite department stores. Earning discounts and being around fashion was a draw for them. As they proved their worth, they have received promotions and full-time employment in significant jobs such as managing, buying, and styling.

While working with a client in the convenience store industry, I learned about an experiment they were conducting using a part-time host at the morning coffee counter in two stores. The job of the host was to warmly greet guests and to fill coffee cups quickly. The objective was to shorten the morning line at the coffee station. It was a rousing success. The company found that the morning rush was filled with regulars who appreciated a familiar face and faster turn-around time. Guess who the hosts were? Retirees who loved interacting with people and earning some extra money. As the program was then rolled out across the company, coffee lines not only moved more quickly, but bottom lines improved as well. The special service resulted in an increase in sales.

There is an organization of retired chief financial officers who freelance their skills by working as "acting" CFOs for small and middle-size companies. They bring a tremendous depth of knowledge to these organizations and play a vital developmental role for them, while at the same time they are able to work a flexible schedule that they set themselves.

MYTHS AND MYSTERIES OF THE OLDER WORKFORCE

There is no mystery to the fact that there are several preconceived notions about the aging population and therefore the aging workforce. The actuality is, however, that these expectations are myths. The older worker brings many more pluses than minuses to the table. Even in the world of advertising, well known for enforcing stereotypes in order to help sell products, the picture of the white-haired couple in rocking chairs has been replaced with images of that same couple golfing, hiking, and enjoying the wonders of Disney World.

In one recent study, employers ascribed several admirable attributes to workers 50 years and older. These strengths include:

- ❑ Experience
- ❑ Commitment to quality
- ❑ Low turnover
- ❑ High level of attendance/punctuality
- ❑ Excellent judgment

You would think that any employer definitely would want people with these kinds of traits on their work force, right? In this same study, however, managers expected certain weaknesses from workers over 50 including: lack of flexibility, inability to learn new skills, lack of physical ability to perform strenuous jobs, and larger health-care costs.[6] For the most part, however, these weaknesses are misperceptions. For example, when employers exclude mid-career and older workers from training, it leads to their inability to perform new jobs. This creates the appearance of inability to adapt. The education level of older workers has actually increased dramatically since 1960, primarily due to the post-baby-boom emphasis on education.

There seems to be little if any evidence linking age and negative job performance. In fact, workers age 55 and above were found to take fewer sick days and to be more loyal to their employers than comparable workers in their 40s. In addition, most jobs don't require strenuous activity. We are finding already that older workers are now concentrated strongly in service industries, as opposed to agriculture or manufacturing where physical strength is a more likely necessity. Finally, research shows that the health-care cost for the final two years of life is less when people live longer. Billions of dollars have been saved as the population in nursing homes has dropped by 200,000 since 1990, even as the number of those age 85 and older has been increasing.[7]

For companies the cost of health insurance should not be an issue in hiring or retaining the older worker. Medicare kicks in at age 65, so older employees will cost less once Medicare becomes their primary coverage. Now that the Medicare prescription plan has been added, once again your older workers will be better taken care of than workers of other ages. Medicare will need to change, since it is predicted to run out of money by 2020, but I expect that health care for the elderly American will become more the responsibility of the government, rather than your company. Therefore, the fact that people are living longer and that their health care is costing more is a national problem to be dealt with, but I don't believe it will cost your company more to employ older workers.

GOOD NEWS! THE EARLY RETIREMENT TREND IS REVERSING

The long-term trend toward early retirement has come to a halt. Until the mid-1980s, there was a significant trend toward earlier retirement among men. It went hand in hand with the excessive workweek—work like the dickens for a few years and then retire early and enjoy life. Commonly cited reasons for the early retirement trend included:

❑ Long-term increase in economic wealth

❑ Expansion of Social Security and employer-sponsored pension plans

❑ Introduction of mandatory retirement rules

❑ The need for business to reduce the number of older, higher paid workers[8]

Since the mid-1980s, the participation rate of older males in the work-force has stabilized (with perhaps even a slight increase) and the workforce participation rate of older females has risen dramatically. Reasons for the halt/reversal of the early retirement trend include:

❑ Mandatory retirement is now illegal in most jobs

❑ Workers are less and less able to depend on Social Security as a primary means of retirement support

❑ Company pension plans are not growing at the rates enjoyed in the past

❑ Both Social Security and private pensions have moved toward age-neutrality, rather than offering incentives at specific ages as they did in the past

❑ Social Security now encourages later retirement

❑ The strong economy from the mid-1980s through the 1990s increased the ease with which displaced workers (fired, etc.) could find replacement jobs[9]

We call this good news for a few reasons. First, when people retire, they need other sources for their income and support. Social Security, pensions, and even the long antiquated, but somehow magical age of 65 for retirement were all designed for a population that was expected to die within just a few years of retirement. Actually, the retirement age of 65 dates from the 1880s, when the famous German statesman, Otto von Bismarck, introduced social insurance in Germany. He determined that the average life expectancy of the adult working male was 67. Then, he figured that if 67 was the average age and the worker made it to age 65, he was entitled to a couple of years off before he died.

Now here we are 130 years later, incredibly still operating within that same framework. As noted earlier in this chapter, life expectancies today extend well beyond 68, but the programs to support retirees haven't expanded to reflect this increased longevity. The trend of the 1980s and 1990s toward early retirement only made things worse. In addition, the volume of the 65 + population is about to increase dramatically, too, with baby boomers poised to enter this age demographic. The first of the boomers will reach age 65 years in 2011.

Second, this is good news because research indicates that ongoing mental and physical activity, such as continuing to work, increases one's health and longevity. So the longer we work, the healthier we stay. Helen Darling, president of the National Business Group on Health, calls retirement the "clicking on of a timer" toward ill health, diminished capacity, and even death. Once employees leave the workforce, they become a drain on society—not only because they don't earn money, but also because the inactivity leads to mental and physical decline.

Finally, this is good news because organizations will need employees in the future, and a growing crop of healthy, willing, and able older workers will be available. The lack of younger replacement workers due to the baby bust that immediately followed the baby boom and the falling fertility rate will increase the need for older workers.

LINKS TO LONGEVITY

Why are we living longer? Just like the age-old balance of nature versus nurture in child rearing, longevity is tied to both genetics and lifestyle choices.

Studies on genes and longevity are seeking genes that promote longer life. In the process, research indicates that those who are genetically predisposed to longer life tend to be very healthy throughout their lives. Thomas Perls, a geriatrician at Beth Israel Deaconess Hospital in Boston, conducted one such study. Research is showing that long-lived people don't have certain genes that pre-dispose certain conditions such as heart disease. In addition, Perls thinks there may be other genes that protect from disease. At any rate, Perls says that most people can have good genes that will help them live long and healthy lives, but that bad habits such as smoking and drinking can un-do the good genes.[10]

More Than Just a Vitamin

In the *New Scientist* edition of July 5, 2003, Nicholas Wald and Malcolm Law of the Wolfson Institute of Preventive Medicine in London proposed the "poly-pill." This is a combination of five inexpensive drugs and the vitamin folic acid in a single pill, which could be offered to everyone over the age of 55. It would address the problems of high LDL ("bad") cholesterol, blood pressure, blood homocysteine levels, and platelet aggregation. Wald and Law claim the "polypill" would cut the chance of heart attacks by 88 percent and strokes by 80 percent. In addition, they predict it would extend the lives of individuals without disease by more than a decade. If these claims prove true, the poly-pill would save almost 800,000 lives a year in the United States alone. Critics charge that giving pills to healthy people to prevent disease has never been tried on such a large scale. Furthermore, they say that some elements contained in the pill can cause internal bleeding, while blood pressure drugs can cause dizziness and fainting. This is a highly controversial issue.[11] Whether this pill is an answer or not, the point is that research continues to deliver life-extending technologies.

Research, however, also indicates that genetics contribute only about 30 percent to life span variations. The choices we make carry the most weight—sometimes literally. This is a very important revelation, because it means that an individual can influence the length of his or her life by making the appropriate lifestyle choices. Historically, the mindset has been that we are "predestined" to certain health concerns, issues, and diseases. Furthermore, the prevailing wisdom held that one's life expectancy could be gauged by checking the biological family tree. We now know that isn't completely true. Lifestyle is a critical factor in longevity. Diet, exercise, social networks, and stress management are viewed as key. Nearly every expert we interviewed and all the research we conducted confirmed that we are largely in charge of our own destiny when it comes to longevity.

Walking Really DOES Clear Your Head

A study released in March, 2004 compared two groups of active seniors. One group was asked to exclusively lift weights as their form of exercise. The other was asked to exclusively pursue cardiovascular exercise, such as jogging or walking on a treadmill. The astounding first- time results show that the walkers/joggers had better mental clarity than those who only lifted weights. Weight lifting, however, is still important to stave off osteoporosis and the like.

TRAITS THAT WILL DEFINE THIS AGING WORK FORCE

The following list of characteristics offer some significant insights into older workers as we consider what longevity will mean to our organizations and plan for the future.

❏ *Older workers are staying put.* Will this huge older population all pick up and move to Florida? According to recent research, this is unlikely. The majority of Americans expect to age in place, growing old in the homes where they currently live.

Fewer people move to retirement communities when they leave their jobs. Americans are less likely to move when they retire than they were in the past. In 1999, fewer than five out of 100 of those 65 and older moved after retirement—that is a smaller number than moved ten years earlier. According to an AARP survey, 89 percent of respondents older than 55 wish to age in place, compared to 84 percent in 1992. This trend will benefit the higher tax, colder weather states of the mid-Atlantic and New England, since retirees tend to spend a lot of money. In balance, however, challenges to public policies will arise. For example, suburban retirees who choose to age in place will need services, such as transportation, home care, and in-home services.

Several kinds of service providers are cropping up to meet the needs of these staying-put seniors. One such example is the Heritage Harper Health Group in Annapolis, Maryland, a nonprofit organization run by its 1,400 members who live in a suburban community. Members pay an $85 membership fee annually, along with charitable contributions that support an administrative staff plus several nurses, and are guaranteed access to a nurse around the clock.[12] In the future, when an aging-in-place population will be available to companies as workers, services needed by them may become perks and incentives to attract this increasingly attractive older workforce.

❑ *As they stay local, older Americans can work for you.* They are available. Moving to Florida implies that the person's inclination is to no longer work, but staying local perhaps implies that they may be willing to continue working.

❑ *For older workers, money may be secondary to social interaction.* For example, the older callers to our 800-service-number love to chat. In this same way, older workers can provide welcomed customer service.

Once while on a business trip in Phoenix, I hailed a taxi and welcomed the air conditioning as I stepped inside. I gave the business address of the prospect that I was visiting. The cab driver was a very attractive older man who chuckled as I gave the name and address. "Is there any information about that company that I can help you with?" he asked. "I used to be the CFO."

"Why are you a cab driver?" I asked incredulously, once I picked my jaw up off the floor. "And, yes, tell me everything you can about the company."

He went on to describe how he had retired two years ago, but was driving his wife crazy with his hanging around the house, so he decided to drive a cab instead. To this man, money was not the draw. He just enjoyed the social interaction of meeting new people. He went on to tell me lots of helpful tips about my prospect. I, in turn, gave him quite a tip as well.

❑ *Older workers see the big picture.* Many times, an experienced employee can see the interactions of various parts of the business that a young one might miss. With experience comes the benefit of "having seen it all before." The older worker, therefore, is less likely to get flustered. They've seen the economy up; they've seen it down. They understand a business cycle that a younger employee hasn't experienced yet. In times of layoffs and downsizing, the older workers are often the calm in the eye of the storm, comforting others with past survival stories.

❑ *Older workers are often extremely well educated.* The Baby Boomers are the most educated workforce in history. As they age, companies will benefit from helpful workers who can train and teach the next generation. At the same time, the Boomers continue to want to learn. Retirees are attending college courses in droves.

❑ *Many older workers have worked in several jobs across the company.* The experience of knowing several jobs at several levels, how they interact, and how they have changed over time is another advantage offered by the older worker. Often, older workers can leverage this broad experience by providing insight into how to make a job better. We have an employee at CGI who has been with us for twenty-six years. Back when we had just three employees, she opened the mail, kept the books, and delivered consulting service. She was there at the onset of the ERISA law, which governs benefits, and she now heads up the department that does government filing for ERISA compliance on behalf of clients. When it comes to ERISA, no one knows more about it or can teach it better. Further, she has been there through all the changes that the law has been through over the years. Her wisdom and continuity in the area are invaluable.

❑ *Older workers possess knowledge of business basics that sometimes seem to elude younger workers.* For example, there are famous sto-

How You Too Can Live Past 100

Compiling data from several sources over several years, I have created the following list. If you include the following in your normal life style, you can increase your life expectancy:

◆ Have a pet, preferably a dog.

◆ Eat breakfast every day.

◆ Get exercise as many days of the week as possible.

◆ Make sure you are volunteering in some capacity.

◆ Have sex at least twice a week. (A person can dream, can't they? Or use this as a homework assignment.)

◆ Lower your blood pressure either through diet and exercise or medication.

◆ Work to make your stress level tolerable and work for you.

◆ Take an aspirin a day, if your doctor approves.

◆ Use dental floss every day. (I bought dental floss stock after seeing this.)

◆ Eat less fat in your diet.

◆ Have faith. (Research is demonstrating that people who believe in a higher power live longer.)

◆ Use seat belts all the time.

◆ Maintain friendships. (Women tend to be better at this than men; so, come on guys, get with the program.)

◆ Don't use a cell phone while driving.

◆ Work on balance through yoga or other exercise programs so you will be less likely to fall. (I started this after my mother's fall.)

◆ Be an optimist.

ries of the high-powered tech companies started by young hotshot computer/software "experts," who have had to hire older workers to run the basic, day-to-day operations of the company. Not surprisingly, these often were the companies that survived when the high-tech bubble burst.

❑ *Older workers make better team players.* Older workers tend to be less competitive with their coworkers. They will be consensus builders. Rather than trying to see their own star rise, because they are past that stage, they are most likely in it for the company—meaning both the business and the social interaction.

❑ *Older workers tend to be less "life" distracted.* Most of the time, their children are grown and out on their own. Their homes are more likely to be paid off. They may be living alone or with a partner, and are at a stage with much less confusion at home. As a result, they have fewer external and homebound forces pulling them and their attention away from work. They can be more focused. They may be more willing to travel or work on special projects. (Of course, at times when a health issue arises, they will need work flexibility or time away from the job.)

❑ *Older workers are more likely to be "self-actualized."* They know who they are, what they are capable of, and what they are good at. Instead of needing constant feedback, they need and want to become coaches. They often have the skills and are not looking for coaching so much as companionship and an avenue to pass along their wisdom. It also follows, then, that older workers may have less need for recognition.

❑ *Older workers are less likely to job hop.* Older workers tend to be more settled. They aren't looking for the fast track. As long as they are treated fairly and with respect, they will tend to stay with one company. When the worker shortage kicks in, seniors will actually help reduce costs because there will be less turnover among them.

CONCLUSION

The aging population of the future will pose challenges and opportunities far beyond pensions and gold watches. They will be a viable and vital constituency of the workforce. How to make sure that these individuals are nurtured for their wisdom, experience, special skills and knowledge, and work ethic in our organizations becomes a critical piece of planning for the future.

Initially, however, there is a philosophical change that needs to take place. At this point, companies need to think through how to revere and fully utilize every employee in every age group, particularly this new population that is aging. They will be healthier; they will be wealthier; they will be wiser. They will have different types of support systems, and most importantly, they will have very different needs from the 20- and 30-somethings that have long been the "brass ring" of employees. The time may soon come when we have a room for employees who take naps in the afternoon. Perhaps we will have elderly people being very productive working a shift that begins at 4:00 or 5:00 A.M. and ends in the early afternoon.

This is the workforce of our future. This is both the challenge and the blessing. We no longer will have a pyramid society with very few elders at the top, but rather a pillar—a pillar of strength for the future.

NOTES

1. Leonard Weiner, "Age Has Its Reward, *U.S. News and World Report*, June 23, 2003, p. 32.

2. Angie Semic Bagley, "Team Member Named Woman of the Year," *Sovereign Today*, May 19, 2002, p.1.

3. The Insider, "No Slowing Down," *Philadelphia Business Journal*, July 11, 2003.

4. John E. Hilsenrath, "Retirees Are Becoming Wealthier, Healthier," *The Wall Street Journal*, May 23, 2001, p. A2.

5. Mary Williams Walsh, "Reversing Decades-Long Trend: Americans Retiring Later in Life," *The New York Times*, February 26, 2001, p. A1.

6. Michael Barth, *An Aging Workforce in an Increasingly Global World* (Binghamton, N.Y.: The Haworth Press, 2000).

7. Milt Freudenheim, "Decrease in Chronic Illness Bodes Well for Medicare Costs," *The New York Times*, May 8, 2001, p. A24.

8. Gary Burtless and Joseph F. Quinn, *Is Working Longer the Answer for an Aging Workforce?: An Issue in Brief.* Center for Retirement Research at Boston College, December 2002: p. 4.

9. Robert Knechtel, "Productive Aging in the 21st Century," *www.go60.com/go60work.htm*.

10. "News from the War Against Death," *Futurific*, September 2001, p. 20.

11. Michael Le Page, "Sheer Brillliance or Utter Madness?" *New Scientist*, July 5, 2003, p. 1.

12. Ibid.

CHAPTER 2

TREND 2: MORE VARIED HOUSEHOLD TYPES

THE FACE OF THE NEW AMERICAN FAMILY

I joined the workforce in 1970 as a young newlywed. My first job was as a recruiter in the HR department of a large bank. My job candidates and new hires were very predictable–white males for management, females for tellers. This was the traditional workforce for my company.

In a rather short time, I moved into the field of benefits and compensation. I remember one of my first benefits design meetings: We were making sure our company benefits were still meeting the needs of the organization and the employees. "No problems here!" chanted the chorus of line managers, as they all nodded their white male heads in unison. At that time, the typical American nuclear family included a male worker/breadwinner, a female stay-at-home caretaker, 2.3 kids, a dog, and a station wagon. Designing benefits was easy . . . one size fit all. We designed all of our benefits to serve perfectly this tradition of Americana. No wonder management thought the benefits were perfect. They were–for them!

Ironically, 80 percent of the employee base at my bank was female, mainly tellers. On the other side of the conference room door, something powerful was happening–and traditional was not going to be typical anymore. At that time, these changes seemed seismic–and they were! However, the situation is even more striking today as the makeup of the American family is changing rapidly, radically, and in a variety of ways not even imagined thirty years ago.

With so many new and varied household types comprising so much of the labor force, companies are no longer able to rely on outdated, nuclear-family stereotypes when shaping their interaction with employees. The more understanding we are of diverse home situations and the more flexible we are in dealing with them, the more we can design human resource policies, benefits plans, and compensation packages to motivate and keep our best workers.

Over and over during interviews for this book, one key to success for organizations in the future resounded clearly: to attract and retain the right team of people. As companies seek to accomplish this, an understanding of new household situations will be critical. As we delve into the research on this topic, we see that companies can no longer assume a "typical" employee's family makeup; it could be very different from their expectations.

THE BREAKDOWN OF NUCLEAR FAMILIES

A traditional family has always meant two married parents of opposite sex and their children. In fewer than fifty years, the number of households made up of a married couple with children under 18 has dropped steeply. In 1960, about 45 percent of all households fit this description. In 2000, for the first time in the history of America, fewer than one in four households were traditional married couples with young children. These so-called traditional households with children under age 18 dropped to 23 percent of all households in 2000.[1]

Thus, the vast majority of households are no longer well served by traditional HR policies, schedules, or benefits. Awareness of this breakdown of the traditional American family is widespread. News media and television sit-com plot lines reinforce the changes every day. Companies are slow to react, however, and their challenge for the future will be to effectively meet the needs of the other 75 percent of their workforce.

Providing benefits to life partners, for example, has been found to increase worker satisfaction and place less strain on health-care services. Controversy abounds over just this one issue, however, and there are no easy answers. Cost is not the only factor. Some consider it a moral issue. Some are caught up in definitions: Who qualifies as life partners? Do they include people in common-law marriages? Same-sex marriages? Significant others who are not married at all? These questions open the door to others who want coverage. I have one friend who wants to include her brother, who is out of work and unmarried, under her health coverage. In her mind, who is more of a partner for life than a brother?

From Family Tree to Family Forest

The breakdown of the traditional family touches everyone, and more than just employers need to react. Creating a family tree has been a popular school assignment for many years. It is no longer so simple. In the United States, the majority of students are not in a traditional family, especially in major metropolitan areas. Students increasingly include children of international adoption, children of gay parents, and children born through advanced reproductive technology. Children of divorce, children with a single parent, children with stepparents and stepsiblings, and children with guardian relatives or foster parents are also common. Some teachers have simply scrapped the family tree assignment from their lesson plans. Others, being more flexible and creative, are asking students to create family time-lines, family orchards, or essays that give children more freedom in telling their personal stories. Companies in the future will be called upon to make the same kinds of creative adjustments.

COUPLES AND MARITAL STATUS

Marital status has long been one of the classic characteristics used to define people in and out of the workforce. Back in the 1950s, this was pretty much represented by "married" or "single"—with the occasional "widow(er)" thrown in. Today, it is not at all unusual to have married couples living separately and single people living together—along with a variety of other living arrangements that stretch the definition of the household in all directions.

HETEROSEXUAL COUPLES

According to the 2000 Census, just over half—52 percent—of all households in the United States include married couples. That means an enormous number of households do not. One reason is that couples today are much more likely to live together without marrying. The social stigma once associated with this as a heterosexual living arrangement has all but disappeared. One sure indication of the former stigma is that "unmarried partner" was not even one of the choices offered prior to the 1990 Census.

Not surprisingly, too, unmarried partners tend to be young. The 2000 Census found that partners in unmarried couple households were an average of twelve years younger than households containing a married couple.

SENIOR DOMESTIC PARTNERS

Another trend that is alive and growing is what my mother would have called "seniors living together without the benefit of clergy." This new type of arrangement works great, often for a widow and widower, or for a group such as "The Golden Girls," sharing a life and supporting each other through good and bad times. My mother described these couples or groups and the wonderful inclusion of them in all functions in her senior community. She said that to be so accepting is a change in her generation's thinking. If the seniors can accept, the employers designing policies and benefits of inclusion can both accept and attract these competent workers with appropriate inclusive policies.

LIVING TOGETHER, ANTICIPATING MARRIAGE

About half of the couples who married in the 1990s lived together first—a dramatic difference even from the hippie era of the 1970s. Looking forward, two-thirds of couples will live together prior to marriage, according to the 2000 Census. Still, most Americans hope to marry at some point and to remain married for life. Census figures back this up—they project that 90 percent of Americans, both men and women, will marry at some point in their lives. With life expectancy at an all-time high, there is no rush.

WAITING FOR MARRIAGE

Women especially, but men as well, today are choosing to marry later and have fewer children than did the baby boom generation. In the United States the average age for a female to get married is 29, and for a male it is

31. In 1950, the median age at marriage was 20 for females, and 23 for men. The reasons that men and women give for these choices are critical for our companies and organizations. Employers who offer benefits that are one-size-fits-all, therefore, will miss the boat. An unmarried twenty-five-year-old may be more interested in training and development than in a big life insurance policy. Companies that have flexible benefits, therefore, will attract this group of young adults (see more in Chapter 8).

There is particular emphasis on career and individuality. Young people want time to develop themselves as individuals before they commit to a partner or to having a child. Financial independence is also important for many, who see it as a prerequisite for marriage or children. Marriage (and children) are viewed as inhibitors of these individual goals. Naomi White, author of *Changing Conceptions: Young People's Views of Partnering and Parenting*, argues that young peoples' attitudes toward marriage result from their "attitude toward their parents' relationship and the parenting they themselves received, as well as their own career, partnering, and parenting expectations."[2] In addition, many people in their twenties are children of divorce; as such, they are often skeptical about marriage and more willing to wait to marry. As your company retools its thinking for the future, it must recognize that the needs of these younger unmarrieds will be different from the past. Things like job advancement, travel, and job satisfaction will be critical components of the employment package.

FEMALE HEADS OF HOUSEHOLD

Today, women are frequently the key drivers and decision makers of their families, whether or not they work outside the home. Still, our society has traditionally awarded the partner who makes the most money with the title "Head of Household." In the future, more and more females will earn the title as well as the responsibility. While only 13 percent of married couple households had a female head of household in the 2000 Census, 46 percent of opposite-sex unmarried couples had a female household head. It's not surprising, therefore, that unmarried household partners are more likely to divide household tasks evenly. Employers who are attentive to the needs of the woman worker with a great deal of financial and household responsibility will be attractive to this new head of household. Picture how holding seminars on financial management, offering assistance finding household help, or providing homework hotlines will be motivating to this employee.

Some Nuggets to Noodle

◆ *Ethnicity and Marriage*—Besides having a young population that is skittish about marriage and taking time to do other things first, ethnicity may play some role in the decision to marry. Native Americans have the highest rate of unmarried partnerships at about 20 percent, followed by African Americans at 17 percent, and then Hispanics, Caucasians, and Asians.

◆ *Geographic Dispersion*—Unmarried partner households are most prevalent in the West, and least prevalent in the South.

◆ *Women Testing Partners*—41 percent of American women between the ages of 15 and 44 have lived, unmarried, with a male partner.

◆ *Most End Up Marrying*—55 percent of unmarried cohabiters end up marrying within five years of living together. Only around 10 percent continue to live together past five years. Of all couples living together, 75 percent say they expect to marry at some point.

SAME-SEX COUPLES

Of the data collected in the 2000 Census on unmarried-couple households, one in nine were partners of the same sex. Slightly more than half of these same-sex households were male partners. Same-sex partnership was, and remains, more common in larger cities. Some companies are clearly ahead of politicians as they offer medical benefits to same-sex couples. The companies are not doing this for social reasons as much as for business reasons. Companies with an open attitude as well as inclusion in major issues such as health and life insurance will be able to attract and retain this group of employees.

WHAT THIS MEANS FOR EMPLOYERS

An employer who recognizes and embraces the change of the nuclear family will attract and retain employees. A recruiter will not be able to guess at an applicant's family situation. The recruiter who can describe a work environment that encompasses the flexibility (including appropriate time off and upward mobility) to support a single head of household or a senior with an unusual nontraditional family will reap the rewards of a robust, high-energy work force.

THE QUESTION OF CHILDREN

Modern day young people appear less confined to the norms and expectations that used to govern our choices. They can choose to marry—or not. They can choose to have children—or not. Still, despite tremendous advances in medical science, a man must either adopt a child or find a surrogate mother to do the actual childbearing for him. While marriage is being redefined in the post-industrial world, from "marriage of convenience" and common law marriage to same-sex marriage, there is also a growing number of ways in which people can create families. Family options both with and without children offer many choices that were previously unavailable. Throughout my research and interviews, I found that there is a keen awareness of this wealth of options. Lifestyle and individual priority have become increasingly important in guiding the decision of whether or not to have children.

Once a couple or an individual decides that they want a child, more options exist than ever before. Adoptions, once secretive, are now quite open. Further, the number of interracial and international adoptions is growing. I know several families who have gone this route and are ecstatic now that they have their children—but the process can be long, cumbersome, and tiring. We have an associate at CGI who has adopted two children from Russia. It was grueling—an emotional, expensive, and time-consuming process for the couple. It included tons of travel, which translated to a lot of time away from work. They were required to bring medical supplies and clothing for the child, as well as gifts and money to "grease palms" along the way. When they finally got their first child—a twelve-month-old girl—she had an ear infection and screamed the entire long 23-hour flight back to the United States.

I have another friend, who, after bearing two biological children, chose to adopt a baby girl from China. In addition to having to go through the same long adoption process, they also had to assimilate a new family member who not only looked different but came from a very different cultural heritage as well.

Companies that can embrace and support their employees in these types of family endeavors, with everything from time-off and understanding to financial assistance, will be the employers of choice as these nontraditional families continue to grow.

Advances in fertility treatments are mind-boggling as well, and open up tremendous opportunities where once there were none. Here, too, forward-thinking employers must be aware of the specific needs of their employees who undertake such procedures—in terms of understanding, as well as providing time away from work, financial support, and medical coverage.

WHAT THIS MEANS FOR EMPLOYERS

These trends toward nontraditional ways of having children hold dramatic implications for employers. We are already seeing a shift toward the availability of parental leave for either parent, not just for mothers. Going forward, however, employees will be faced with many more issues around the processes of having children. As mentioned, international adoptions often require that the parents spend several weeks in the native land of the child before they can bring the child home. Then there are the costs—who pays for what? If you have a baby through a routine pregnancy, health insurance typically pays. Should health insurance, therefore, cover in-vitro fertilization and other medical fertility treatments? For adoptions things can get even stickier. The cost of airplane fares, hotel stays, paper work, and legal fees all add up considerably—and employees are more likely to apply pressure to their employers to help pay the bills.

Even with traditional pregnancies, medical costs are rising in response to the "waiting game" discussed earlier in this chapter. As many more women wait to have children, high-risk pregnancies are on the rise. The number of women between age 40 and 44 who are choosing to give birth has increased by 23 percent since 1995, according to the 2000 Census. Above age 35, women are considered to have high-risk pregnancies regardless of their health. High-risk implies the need for more tests and more careful monitoring throughout the pregnancy, which means more costs.

The 2000 Census also shows there is also a growing trend of unmarried couples having children. From 1996 to 2002, the number of married households with children under age 18 grew 3 percent. During the same period, the number of unmarried partners with children under age18 grew 39 percent. Again, this offers employers both challenges and opportunities as they consider what financial coverage and time off they will provide.

SINGLE-MOTHER HOUSEHOLDS

While the number of children living with a single mother has grown substantially, much of that can be attributed to population increases over the last thirty years. There has been enormous growth in the number of single mothers who have never married; they account for 42 percent of all single-mother families. This new trend decreases the percentage of widowed mothers and married mothers whose spouse is absent.

Single mothers have been a part of the workforce for many years, and a great many employers have already taken steps to allow special work schedules, time-off when needed, and other considerations. Once again, it would be wise for all companies to accommodate single mothers where possible, since they are often the most productive and loyal employees you will find anywhere. A bit of time lost here and there will be repaid many times over.

Single-Mother Communes

There is an interesting trend toward the creation of live-in support networks—single mothers sharing homes with other single mothers to lighten the financial and parenting burden. Co-abode.com is a Web site that helps connect these single parents to become roommates. Generally, the mothers who are trying this see the pros as outweighing the cons. It makes single-family homes a more viable option when more than one salary is contributing to the mortgage. These single parents share chores as well as stresses and experiences, and they have fewer babysitting hassles. Do I even need to mention that these types of arrangements can ease the demands for support from employers? Perhaps instead, forward-thinking and involved employers will provide an information network for employees looking to try this kind of arrangement.

SINGLE-FATHER HOUSEHOLDS

While their total number is still small, the fastest growing household type is the single male head of household. According to the 2000 Census, single men are raising children in 2.2 million households. This represents a 62 percent increase since 1990. Single fathers have been found to earn substantially less than married fathers. This lower household income is coupled with a tendency for single fathers to be less educated and more in need of public support than married fathers, a socio-economic gap that has been increasing since 1984. While single fathers are certainly not limited to poorer and less educated, the trend indicates a challenge for employers who may be called upon to support these households in new ways.

For over ten years, we at CGI had a wonderful employee named Nina, who helped our clients' employees every time they hit a wall on a health-care claim. She was their tireless advocate. Often Nina was described as "a fierce dog that wouldn't let go of the bone" in fighting to recover insurance money. Nina was diagnosed with breast cancer when she was pregnant with her second child and when her first child was four years old. She fought the disease valiantly for two years—and continued working on clients' behalf even from her hospital bed. In the end, however, her husband became a single father, raising a two- and a six-year-old. Imagine the patience and support he will require of an employer going forward—from providing emotional space to time away from work.

GRANDPARENTS AS PRIMARY CAREGIVERS/GUARDIANS

According to the 2000 Census, nearly 5 percent of all children live in the homes of their grandparents; for 35 percent of those children the grandparents are the primary caregivers. These percentages have remained constant over the past few decades. As we know from Chapter 1, the face of today's grandparent is different. Not only does it look different (with or without plastic surgery), but most likely the lifestyle is more active. These grandparents may be at a better age to care for young children now than if they had their children at a young age. Still, it may be a hardship for some grandparents, particularly if they are older or have financial difficulties.

If the grandparents, whether of middle age or older, are still working, it is a challenge for both the employer and employee. Employers who provide support systems, day care, or flexible time will be important to this group.

GAY PARENTS

A growing numbers of same-sex couples are choosing to include children in their families. According to the 2000 Census, 33 percent of female couples and 22 percent of male couples have children living with them.

The increasing number of ways that children can join families bolsters this trend. Adoption and foster parenting, traditionally available only to married couples, are becoming more open to same sex-couples as well as singles. Biomedical advances enhance opportunities as well. Donor insemination, artificial insemination, and surrogate births are becoming more common options. Dubbed the "gayby boom," gay couples are having families even without the kinds of legal protection heterosexual married couples enjoy. Options for gay men wanting to be parents include foster-care and, more recently, surrogacy, which can cost between $50,000 and $90,000. This is an area where gay employees could be looking for some assistance from their employers.

SUPPORT NETWORKS FOR PARENTS

With all of these variations of family, the phrase "It takes a village to raise a child" becomes ever more relevant these days. Both households where two partners work and single- parent households continue to grow in record numbers. As such, finding a support network outside the home becomes critical.

Thanks in no small part to the increase in healthy longevity, grandparents are often the first up to the plate. Beyond the grandparents who are actually rearing their grandchildren, as discussed above, other grandparents are a common support network solution. Grandparents who serve as the number-one babysitter are only the beginning. I know of several young families where both parents or the single parent work, and who rely on grandparents to serve as after-school care providers, as emergency contacts who are closer to school, and even as live-in support. I have one young acquaintance, a single mom who works full-time, whose mother has lived with her since her divorce several years ago and who helps rear her son. In several families I know, the grandmother arrives Sunday night and leaves on Friday, and this has been their solution for years.

Overall, women are more adept than men at developing an effective support network. They are generally more likely to reach out to peers, neighbors, or even church associates for help. Support systems have been found to be stronger if they include friends. One study of inner-city minority women found that they are more likely to suffer from physical illness, psychological illness, and stress than inner-city men, and that this is especially true if their support networks are weak. Support systems are viewed as weak if they are composed only of neighbors or family members, but include no friends. The availability of friends in a support network implies a freedom to choose, thus the situation is less desperate.

Still, women are better equipped to develop effective support networks than men are. "Our studies have shown that among married moms, single moms, married dads and single dads, single fathers were less satisfied with their child care arrangements" says Dr. Carol Erdwins, clinical psychologist at George Mason University.[3] Single fathers, especially, do not have the same social support from other fathers that single mothers do. This will increasingly provide employers with a unique way to support their male employees.

COMPANY SUPPORT SYSTEMS

Dr. Louis Buffardi, professor of industrial and organizational psychology at George Mason University, concludes, "Allowing employees to have greater control over the workday, is perhaps the best way a company can assist with child care responsibilities."[4] His studies have shown that if companies are sensitive to employees' childcare issues, employees in turn will perceive that the organization really does care about their well-being. This leads to a wide variety of positive outcomes for the company.

As this growing number and variety of household types reach a critical mass, businesses will need to step up to the plate in providing services to support parents. Giving employees greater control over their workday is the simplest way to achieve this. To date, this kind of employee control comes mainly at a cost to women, who are forced to downshift their jobs, or at least their career expectations, and then fight like the devil to gain a special arrangement to accommodate their home/life needs. These situations are often accompanied by sideways glances, office gossip, and the expectation that work will suffer. Usually, however, these women are even more loyal to their employers and more productive in exchange for being able to maintain a balance with their family life.

In the future, employers need to become proactive in making available employee control and flexibility as much as possible—to reach out to their employees, especially perhaps to single fathers who may be hesitant to seek support from their employer. So many solutions exist—they need only be embraced. Job sharing can work very well in positions that require a constant hands-on presence. Virtual offices are growing in popularity as technology becomes both affordable and refined.

This kind of flexibility works. For example, Linda Rosanio, CEO of The STAR Group in Cherry Hill, New Jersey, allows technology and trust to bridge the gap between workers and their children. Laptop computers, teleconferencing, and e-mail connections to home give the company's working mothers greater flexibility and control. Results have been great. Clients are happy. Work is getting done. Children have a parent to meet them when they get off the bus after school.

Flexibility will become the norm, not the exception. Obviously, families and households no longer fit into traditional molds. However, even within this diverse universe, ever-wider variety appears every day. Therefore, the emphasis must be on flexibility—and employers must look at each situation individually.

Moms in Government

The recent spate of female senators with young children is a new phenomenon with a wonderful potential to effect positive change. Before 1992, there were no mothers with children at home serving in the U.S. senate. In 2003, there are fourteen female senators—four with children of school age or younger. These women—as well as male senators with young children—are balancing parenting and career in the same work-home balancing act that most parents have practiced for years. They are able to get the ear of their male peers in ways that the all-male Congressional club of the past could not. They have certain credibility, say their male colleagues, on matters that affect women in the workplace.

It is not an easy career choice for a mother. Both senator and mom are 24/7 jobs. Congressional schedules can change moment to moment. Sometimes votes take place in the middle of the night. In addition, senators work in two places: the U.S. Capitol and their home state. Finally, though, parents are finding champions in the government, and senators who are working mothers are making subtle headway.

For example, female senators have pressed the majority leader to refrain from holding voting sessions during the dinner hour. It seems almost crazy that this had become part of the senate routine. To my mind, it reflects what Molly D. Shepard, founder of The Leaders Edge, an organization dedicated to enhancing women's effectiveness as senior leaders, called the "race to see who ISN'T going to the elevator," where success equals working long hours. Women are not the only ones who are fed up with unreasonable and unrelenting work hours. This new movement has won the quiet support of Congressional men, as well, who would also like to have dinner with their children.

COUNTERTREND—TRADITIONAL FAMILIES FOR THE NEW MILLENNIUM

In many ways, the younger generation is more prepared for, and comfortable with, nontraditional gender roles. Take, for example, the twenty-two-year-old college senior who says, "I would be 100 percent satisfied if my wife made enough money so I could be a stay-at-home dad." Still, there is a countertrend to the increasing number of different household types—a return to tradition. Old gender roles die hard, and many find that, particularly when it comes to children, the Ozzie and Harriet model often is still preferable. This is especially true for young males. Young men are more likely to be in favor of traditional gender roles in parenting. Young women are more likely to react negatively to this expectation. Consider these quotes:

❏ *From a twenty-five-year-old female*: "I have met more men who want to be fathers than women who want to be mothers, because I think women have more to lose."

❏ *From a twenty-two-year-old male*: "I think that a woman would be more committed to parenting of a child, because there is more of that closeness. Having been pregnant and giving birth to the child and all that sort of thing. There is a closer bond."[5]

By and large, gender roles and expectations have been found to reflect the way one was raised. Even though the number of stay-at-home dads and single fathers is growing, it is still very small. Most children still experience the mother as the primary caregiver. These expectations then form part of the basic fiber of the next generation. As such, young women expect that the bulk of childcare and domestic responsibilities will be on their shoulders and that they will need to sacrifice their careers as a result. Young men agree and feel that the burden of making enough money to support the family falls to them.

In this countertrend, then, we see a resurgence of the traditional family with a stay-at-home mom, but with a twist for the new century. The homemakers do more than make cookies. They function as business mentors, financial advisers, confidants, and even as additional income producers. The push toward family values supports this trend, as does the push to regain balance in one's life. More and more families are willing to sacrifice income and luxury to gain time for and control of their home life. Many dual-income families are finding that they can reduce or even drop one salary and still live quite comfortably.

Finally, the unfortunate view of divorce as an easy solution, best for all concerned, even including the children, seems to be changing. Long-term studies that followed children of divorce for as long as twenty-five years are finding compelling data in favor of staying married for the sake of the children. Divorce appears to have an effect on the children's future relationships. One study, described in the book *The Unexpected Legacy of Divorce: A 25-Year Landmark Study*, found that 40 percent of children of divorce never married. Others married badly, making rash decisions and poor choices. In contrast, the study found that marriages that were maintained showed children that families are a safe place, where disagreements happen and can be resolved without pulling the family apart.[6]

CONCLUSION: FLEXIBILITY AND RESPECT RULES

Resurgence of tradition aside, the overall trend is very clear. The future holds no specific typical family. The traditional family that some of us grew up with will no longer dominate.

Companies must think through and adapt policies to reflect the wide variety of needs of the growing spectrum of household types. What we can do to attract and retain our employees is to be aware of how different their home life might be from what we think it might be. We can make no assumptions based on history, but rather we must make assumptions based on knowing that the trend is toward an increasing variety of household types. Each of these household types is a family unit in its own right, whether or not it is different from what the law recognizes as a family. Whomever it includes, family is just as important as ever to the employee. In the future, our employee benefits, policies, compensation, relocation packages, and work schedules need to reflect flexibility and respect for any household type.

NOTES

1. Eric Schmitt, "For the First Time, Nuclear Families Drop Below 25 Percent of Households," *The New York Times*, May 15, 2001, p. A1.
2. Naomi Rosh White, "Changing Conceptions: Young People's Views of Partnering and Parenting," *Journal of Sociology*, June 2003, p. 149.
3. Louis Buffardi, "Single Fathers in the Workforce: Growing in Numbers," *Society for Industrial and Organizational Psychology*, March 7, 2003.
4. Ibid.
5. White, "Changing Conceptions," p. 149.
6. Judith Wallerstein, *The Unexpected Legacy of Divorce: A 25-Year Landmark Study* (New York: Hyperion Press, 2000).

CHAPTER 3

TREND 3: GENERATIONS

BOOMERS AND ECHOS AND NEXTERS—OH MY!

When I got married more than twenty-five years ago, I was shocked by the number of socks my husband brought with him. He cleared out two or three drawers and filled them with socks. Some of them had never been opened and still had tags on them; others had tremendous holes. Being the new and doting wife, I sorted the socks—matched sizes and colors, tossed the "holey" ones, unwrapped the new ones. Big mistake! Bob loved his socks—ALL of them—and I wasn't to throw out a single one. Over the years, Bob's socks have become a running family joke, but the root of the attachment is quite clear. Raised during the depression, he had to wash out his socks each night and keep wearing them over and over again. This was the first time the differences in generations hit home for me—we are shaped by the experiences we live through. Separated by nearly sixteen years, my husband and I are from two different generations. He was eight years old when America was stunned by the attack on Pearl Harbor, December 7, 1941. It was a day that had a tremendous impact on him and has shaped his values and priorities even today.

I, on the other hand, am a Baby Boomer, a label I've always hated. Still, it meant that I always had enough socks and never kept or attempted to darn a "holey" one. Pearl Harbor was a chapter in my history book. I did, however, grow up with the belief that holding a textbook over my head while I crouched under my desk at school would keep me safe from the Russian threat of a nuclear bomb. The assassinations of John F. Kennedy,

Martin Luther King, Jr., and Robert Kennedy were life-shaping historic moments for me.

For my daughter's generation, socks are important only as a fashion statement and they probably never heard of the word "darn" in reference to a sock. At twenty-one, my daughter is part of a new generation that seems to care very deeply about the future of our world. Their historical markers include the explosion of the space shuttle Columbia (though they don't remember the 1986 Challenger explosion), the war in Iraq, and most significantly, the terrorist attacks on the World Trade Center and Pentagon on September 11, 2001.

So, using my little family as a springboard, I can readily identify the significance and potential of three generations. At the same time, I realize that we are not only a product of our home environment and heredity but also of the historical context of our upbringing.

In the future, successful organizations will find the different generations more relevant than ever. Why? In short, because they are all working and will continue to do so. For the first time in our history, four generations are active in the workforce at one time. They are, in fact, working together, interacting in the workplace. It's not just old man Jones sitting up in the executive suite and young Billy down in the mailroom, never to cross paths. Billy is probably up in Mr. Jones' office, helping him set up his computer to retrieve specific data he needs every day. As I am finding in so many areas, old paradigms of thinking are just that: old—and outdated. They will not work in the future.

In the past, companies could put generations into three tidy little groups, each with its own area of focus:

- ❑ *The Older Generation*: retired or getting ready to retire and concerned with their pensions
- ❑ *The Middle Generation*: the bulk of the workforce focused primarily on benefits and compensation
- ❑ *The Younger Generation*: the workforce of future, in need of training and education

Think about it. Many companies solved most of their workforce issues within these three silos. Need to shake things up? Save some money? Get rid of the "dead wood" and have an early retirement drive. Want to motivate your workers? Give them "family friendly" benefits and an annual picnic. Want to whip those up-and-comers into shape and attract the best and the brightest at the same time? Put together a management training program, complete with lectures, guest speakers, and job rotations. It was so easy, wasn't it? Now look! People are working who are 20, 40, 60, and even 80. It's all getting so complicated—or is it?

In the future, companies will face many generations active in the work-force simultaneously, thanks mainly to increased longevity and people look-ing to remain on the job years past what used to be considered retirement age. How will companies need to adjust their human resource functions—from recruiting and training to benefits and compensation—based on the different needs and expectations of the different generations? If they are looking to develop satisfied, productive workforces blending a wide variety of skills and experiences—which, of course, they should be—companies will start answering these questions today.

In this chapter, I will define the generations, delve a little deeper into what makes them tick, and then look at the implications for employers of these generations all working together. According to the book *Generations at Work* by Ron Zemke, Claire Raines, and Bob Filipczak:

> The three generations that occupy today's workplace and the fourth generation that is entering it are clearly distinguish-able by all these criteria—their demographics, their early life ex-periences, the headlines that defined their times, their heroes, music, and sociology, and their early days in the workplace. Their differences can be a source of creative strength and a source of opportunity, or a source of stifling stress and unrelent-ing conflict. Understanding generational differences is critical to making them work for the organization and not against it. It is critical to creating harmony, mutual respect, and joint effort where today there is suspicion, mistrust, and isolation.[1]

DEFINING THE GENERATIONS

Here is a thumbnail sketch of each of the major generations of today. I found some differences in birth years attributed to each, so I took the most common or that used by the Census Bureau. All the names, nicknames, birth years, and overlap became confusing. Laying it out this way was helpful to me. Consider it as a vertical timeline.

The Silent Generation
- Born 1922 to 1945
- Key Influences: The Great Depression and the New Deal; World War II; Holocaust; Hiroshima; radio and movies.
- Other Names: The Veterans; Seniors; The Greatest Generation.

The Baby Boomers
- Born 1946 to 1964
- Key Influences: Vietnam War; assassinations of JFK, Martin Luther King, Jr., and Robert Kennedy; putting a man on the Moon; Watergate; Cold War and bomb shelters; television; women's liberation, sexual revolution; environmental concerns (Green Party, Exxon Valdez).
- Other Names: Boomers; "Me" Generation.

Generation X
- Born 1965 to 1976
- Key Influences: Demolition of the Berlin Wall; Challenger disaster; Clinton sex scandal; the skyrocketing growth of the stock market and the abundant economy in the 1980s and 1990s; 24-hour live, remote news coverage; the dot-com economy; hi-tech start-ups.
- Other Names: Baby Bust; Xers.

Baby Boom Echo
- Born 1977 to 2000
- Key Influences: Oklahoma City bombing; Rodney King beating; O.J. Simpson trial; Columbine High School massacre; Y2K; Internet; September 11, 2001 terrorist attacks; corporate scandals (Enron); video games; instant messaging.
- Other Names: Generation Y; Nexters; Internet Generation; Millennials (for those born in the 1980s and 1990s).

Millennium Generation
- Born Since 2000
- Key Influences: Yet to be determined.

   ✦ Other Names: I call this generation the Millennials. I feel that twenty years is a large span for one generation and I want to make the point that children who are just coming into the world with the new century will have their own set of influences. These babies will be the ones living the trends we are predicting now. This generation, and the one yet to come, will be the workforce that picks up where the Boomers leave off.

How Generations Enhance Understanding

There are varying views about whether understanding the generations is a useful tool for understanding what motivates an individual. Both sides of the argument make relevant points. On the one hand is the argument that factors other than birth year have a major impact on who one is: upbringing, education, affluence or lack of it, and even geography, just to name a few. I agree. On the other hand, members of a generation do share a history that reflects the news, views, politics, and entertainment that shaped their youth. I think both influences are relevant.

For employers, however, generations are perhaps the most consistent indicator of work needs. While a person can move, get an education, or change financial circumstances, a birth date never changes. It is a useful and dependable benchmark for certain information and is critical for longitudinal studies and trends. Companies and coworkers alike benefit from an understanding of the characteristics of the generations.

People born in the same generation have shared experiences that influence their perceptions and priorities and that shape who they are. They share the historic events, economics, and culture of their time. For example, members of the Silent Generation may remember going to bed hungry, or, similarly to my husband, not having enough socks. They remember the attack on Pearl Harbor as a cataclysmic event beyond anything they could imagine. They also grew up in a time when holding hands on a date was a really big deal. As a result, they bring a certain set of principles and priorities to work. We call them the Silent Generation because they pretty much would "put up and shut up." They could remember things much worse than anything they were facing in the workplace. They were duty bound and loyal to their employers because people generally worked in one place for life.

Recognizing these key commonalities for a given generation helps guide employers as they seek to attract, retain, and support them as employees. This does not mean buying into and reinforcing stereotypes about the different age groups; it does mean having a basic understanding of the forces and influences that helped shape each generation and being aware of the needs and concerns of each group. As always, each employee is an individual and should be treated as such.

DELVING A LITTLE DEEPER INTO THE GENERATIONS

In order to understand this trend and what it will mean for employers, we have to take a closer look at each of the generations outlined above:

THE SILENT GENERATION: BORN 1922 TO 1945

Let's put the country's most mature generation in perspective. According to Louis Pol, demographer and associate dean of the College of Business Administration at the University of Nebraska at Omaha, the birthrate was fairly stable early in the 20th century. Then, during the Great Depression and World War II, the birthrate declined. At the same time, though, we had massive migrations from Europe to the United States. During these times, people knew greater economic turmoil and hardship than any American generation before or since. They survived through self-discipline, sacrifice, and pure hard work. The New Deal made construction workers out of many who had previously held jobs in other professions. The war led women to join the assembly lines of American factories. After the war, this generation enjoyed, albeit conservatively, a life of steadily increasing affluence and luxury.

The Silent Generation is the most traditional: working fathers, nuclear families, and traditional work ethics. They tend to be highly disciplined, hardworking, and loyal employees who play by the rules. They are the wisdom-keepers of America. They have so much to offer all of the generations—where America came from and what our elders endured to give us all that we take for granted today.

Even if they do not hold managerial positions, many of these senior employees are natural workplace leaders. They know how things are done—and why. They can assist younger workers in finding information they need or in determining who is the right person to go to in a given situation. Much of this type of knowledge is not written down in employee handbooks and job descriptions—it is simply woven into the fabric of a workplace. Still, it is vital in maintaining a thriving team atmosphere.

A natural affinity is developing between this generation and the Baby Boom Echo Generation. The indication for employers is that a mentor relationship between a Senior and an Echo would be a good match. While the Silent Generation has felt undervalued for quite a while, it seems that the tide is turning and that they are becoming open to remaining at work (or coming back to the work place after they reach retirement age) if given adequate flexibility.

THE BABY BOOMERS: BORN 1946 TO 1964

At the end of the World War II, we enjoyed an economic boom. It was a time of optimism and industry and growth. Spurred on by returning veterans, the large influx of immigrants, and the general sense of optimism pervading the country, we made babies like crazy. In her article "Generational Divide," Alison Stein Wellner says that America was "in the mood" to make babies after World War II.[2] (If you get the reference to Glenn Miller, give yourself an extra credit point.) During the Baby Boom years, there were more than 75 million births. What's more, each year the birthrate increased over the preceding year until 1964. From 1946 to 1964, there were over 4 million births per year in the United States—that is the definition of the Baby Boom.

The Baby Boom Generation took the steadily increasing affluence that their parents were enjoying after World War II and ran with it. That was their parents' plan—to create the opportunity for their children to have more than they did. Education became a top priority. Many of the Boomers were raised in homes enjoying economic prosperity and a strong nuclear family. Most of their mothers were homemakers; most of their fathers were the family breadwinners.

The Boomers are an interesting group. The sheer size of the group means that society goes where they go. Perhaps the "Silent" Generation just can't be heard above the roar of the Boomers.

The Boomers gave us hippies, communes, and free love. They also gave us the 80-hour workweek. Although generally seen as self-absorbed,

Boomers are active in social issues, civil rights, and politics. They are an optimistic, competitive group that focuses deeply on personal accomplishment.

Three in One: Dissecting the Baby Boom

The Baby Boom is often viewed as three generations in one. The leading edge of the Baby Boom, the first six years, came after a much lower birth generation, but in big-growth, high-optimism years. That group was able to study whatever they wanted in college, or even to get good jobs without attending college. They were able to burn their bras, burn the flag, burn their draft cards, burn their brains on drugs, take a couple of years off to find themselves and come back to get a good job.

The next seven years make up the middle of the Baby Boom. These middle Boomers had a very different situation—they could not get good jobs as easily because the older Boomers had clogged the pipeline. They had to have strong, clean transcripts and not take a lot of chances if they wanted to get the same good jobs that the leading edge of the Baby Boom had coasted into.

The tail end, the last five years of the Baby Boom, had a completely different set of circumstances. These late Boomers were at a disadvantage. They had a huge number of Boomers ahead of them in the workforce moving up into middle management. There was no place for the tail end to go. They had to settle for jobs that people previously started right out of high school, except now they needed a college degree to land these jobs. Also prices had greatly escalated for basics, such as housing. The Late Boomers did not have the same sense of entitlement. They had to have an MBA to get that same job that the leading edge of the Boom could have gotten right out of college or maybe even high school. As futurist Edie Weiner puts it, "If you think that the Baby Boom is one generation from beginning to end, then you think Peter, Paul, and Mary, and Metallica are cut from the same cloth, and they clearly aren't, right?"[3]

A recent book by Jonathan Pontell sought to break out the last piece of the Baby Boom into a distinct segment he coined "Generation Jones." He defines this generation as those born from 1954 to 1965. In his view, this generation is too young for the Baby Boom and too old for the Baby Bust/Generation Xers. While some are agreeing with him, others say that his views are just typical of the Baby Boom—self-focused, wanting special recognition.

Bound by Values

Ken Dychtwald, president of Age Wave, is one of the nation's leading authorities on the Baby Boom. While acknowledging differences among the Boomers, he likens them to a forest of trees sharing the same root system. "Boomers are an extremely diverse generation, an extraordinarily complex yet individualistic collection of men and women," he says. "But under the surface, we're a generation with many, many common values and experiences. We're bound together by deeply rooted values." According to Dychtwald, these values include a belief in meritocracy, a respect for knowledge, and a lack of respect for authority.[4]

Boomers and Finances

An interesting debate rages over the amount of money that will be passed down to the Boomers from their Silent Generation parents. One school of thought is that this will determine how long the Boomers will stay working. There are some 50 million Silent Generation Americans, and they are the wealthiest group of seniors in U.S. history. Estimates are that they control as much as two-thirds of the country's financial assets—including 40 percent of the mutual funds, 60 percent of the annuities, and 48 percent of luxury cars. Still, with all this wealth, the amount earmarked for inheritance is dwindling on a couple of fronts. First, the Silent Generation is facing unprecedented health-care costs and other expenses. Second, as they live longer and better, the Silent Generation is less willing to sock it away for their children. In the early 1990s, 56 percent of those over age 65 felt it was important to leave an inheritance. By 2000, that figure had dropped to less than half, 47 percent. This is credited not only to increased life expectancy and rising expenses, but also to a realization that their children are doing even better than they did.

At the same time, Boomers are notoriously poor savers. The Me Generation spends, spends, spends. They buy more products and services than any other generation. They may need that inheritance when it's all said and done.

They have time to start saving, though. Boomers are entering their Golden Age according to sociologists. The positions they hold, the money they make, and the achievements they can attain are just reaching their peak.

How Long Will the Boomers Work?

Boomers will continue to work far beyond what was traditionally considered retirement age. In spite of the fact that many people attribute this to the Boomers' lack of savings, I believe that, in large part, they will continue to work because they want to work. Boomers are so driven to succeed that I cannot imagine that they will settle down and do nothing for the last twenty-five or thirty years of their life. They would get too bored.

I do see them working at something they enjoy, however. After driving themselves to tension headaches and high blood pressure for the first half of their career, the Boomers will seek employment that better aligns with their dreams and aspirations. In addition, the Baby Boom includes the first generation of professional career business women, many of whom will just be hitting their stride in their fifties and beyond. I believe a large number of smart, skillful businesswomen will be rejoining the workforce once their own children have grown. While as many as one in three Boomers say they would stop working if they could afford it, I'm not sure that this will be the reality.

At the same time, the Boomers will move toward better balance between work and home. Many are willing to trade higher pay for more time for themselves and their families. This is a trend we are seeing across the generations, a trend that is gaining support and momentum. Boomers, given their propensity to spend and self-focus, are expected to increase their travel and recreational activities as a means to enhance their work–life balance. They will be less stressed, hopefully, and bring a more balanced, patient perspective to their jobs. In addition, they will gain insight, appreciation, and a broader view as a result of seeing places other than their office and doing things other than their work. After all, this is the group that gave us the term "workaholic," and most "-aholics" need the help of a twelve-step program to get control.

Bookend Boomers

Sometimes called the Bookend or Sandwich generation, Boomers are surrounded by issues from elder parents on one end and children in their twenties on the other. Young adult offspring continue to put demands on their time and energy, demands that the Boomers themselves never would have thought to make of their own parents. At the same time, more and more Boomers are being put in the position of needing to parent their parents, who are elderly and in declining health. This will be relevant to employers whose Boomer employees face stresses, time demands, and money constraints, all of which require company support and understanding.

GENERATION X: BORN 1965 TO 1976

Douglas Coupland first coined this label in his book *Generation X*. When the book was written in 1992, Generation Xers were " twenty-something." Now many of them are well into their thirties. Generation X is fascinating. On one hand, it is considered a generation raised with even more of a silver spoon and a sense of entitlement and much less political interest than the Baby Boomers. As a result, they are often viewed as slackers with less involvement in, and more pessimistic views about, politics and other issues. On the other hand, some Xers are hard-core traditionalists—optimistic and hardworking. Some are like a second wave of hippies and some are narrow-minded believers in gender roles and stereotypes. Generation X, more than any other generation I studied, is the one most that is elusive because the differences among its members can be so extreme. In many cases, the labels ascribed to them are not only too general, they are outright wrong.

Generation X is also the group most attached to (or blamed for) the dot-com fury and the stock market boom days of the 1980s and 1990s. According to Benjamin Soskis, this is largely a misperception. Fewer than 5 percent of Gen Xers are employed in computer-related industries. Moreover, a 1998 investor study by the Investment Company Institute found that the median stockholding of Xers was $20,000 and the median age for investors was 47, i.e., more Boom than Bust.

Fifty-one million Americans are considered members of Generation X. Just like those generations that came before them, Xers grew up in a different world. The divorce of their parents has often been cited as the event having the single greatest impact upon them. The high rate of divorce and increased number of working mothers led to Xers being the first generation of latch-key kids. As a result, traits of independence, resilience, and adaptability are often among their attributes.

Generation X feels strongly that they do not need someone looking over their shoulder. They also desire immediate and on-going feedback and are equally comfortable giving feedback to others. Other traits of this group include working well in multicultural settings, desire for some fun in the workplace, and a pragmatic approach for getting things done.

Generation X also saw their parents get laid off and face job insecurity in a way that previous generations never did. They have redefined loyalty. Instead of remaining loyal to their employer, they have a commitment to the work–to the teams with whom they work and to the bosses for whom they work.

BABY BOOM ECHO: BORN 1977 TO 2000

By 1977, many Boomers decided to have children, and the birthrate began to climb again. This created a surge in the population and a generation called the Baby Boom Echo. I found many different starting and ending years attributed to the Baby Boom Echo–beginning anywhere from 1976 to 1982 and ending around 1994 to 2001.

The Baby Boom Echo is entering the workforce now and will be coming on in force through the first quarter of the 21st century. Nearly 75 million strong, this generation is coming of age as powerful and positive. Their parents, the Boomers, are seen as the most child-centered caregivers in American history. This brings us to another label–the Soccer Mom. Parents of the Echo are shuttling their children everywhere–soccer, softball, karate, dance, tutors, singing, and piano–and that's just one child! With the taxi service come high expectations of achievement, as the highly competitive Boomer parents see their children as both an extension and a reflection of themselves. It seems that even when it comes to parenting, the Boomers are all about "me." At any rate, the Baby Boom Echo is seen as a largely self-confident group, sometimes even cocky. They like to set goals and go for them. Since they have had to be good at time management since day one, Echos are multitaskers and team players. In fact, they typically prefer to work in groups rather than alone. They also tend to socialize in groups rather than as couples.

High-tech is second nature to them. Many of the Echos have never seen a dial phone and cannot imagine that we saw *The Wizard of Oz* only once a year. In spite of the showers of attention they received, they do expect to work hard. They desire structure and direction in the workplace. Perhaps as a result of years of having coaches and head-strong parents, the Echos are respectful of positions and titles and desire a relationship with their boss. This may not always sit well with Generation X, who are largely hands-off, independent workers. On the other hand, the Echo is the group, as I mentioned before, that is expected to work very well with the Seniors.

One reason for this affinity may be the hardships witnessed by the Baby Boom Echo. In between soccer and softball, this generation saw parents lose their jobs in record numbers due to lay-offs and "right-sizing." The Echos saw retirees struggling to get by, and seniors taking jobs at McDonald's to make ends meet. The recession of the late 1990s and into the 2000s brought an abrupt end to the Roaring '80s and '90s, similar to the abrupt end of the Roaring '20s. Another interesting commonality between the World War II generation and the Baby Boom Echo is their faith in the military. A poll for the Harvard Institute of Politics finds that 75 percent of 1,200 undergraduates surveyed report trusting the military "to do the right thing" all or most of the time.[5]

Encouraging the Connection

Hewlett-Packard (HP) is one company that is taking advantage of the natural affinity between the Silent Generation and the Baby Boom Echo. In 1995, the company began a mentoring program pairing HP employees with thousands of middle- and high-school students. Primarily through the use of e-mail communication, the program is credited with having a tremendous positive impact on the students.

Employers are already looking forward to getting the rest of the Baby Boom Echo into the workforce, expecting this large and positive group to change society for the better and increase productivity. Echos are generally found to be more favorable about their work situation and to feel that management has a clearly communicated vision. They are looking for guidance, and 75 percent report that their managers are available when needed.[6] They are also expected to be fiercely loyal to managers whom they trust to teach and nurture them—much as they trusted their coaches.

According to the book *Generations at Work*, by Ron Zemke, Claire Raines, and Bob Filipczak, seven attributes characterize the Baby Boom Echo:

1. Their supervisory style is not fixed. How closely they monitor and manage, for instance, is a product of each individual's track record and personal preferences. Control and autonomy are a continuum, not solitary options.

2. Their leadership style is situationally varied. Some decisions are consensually made; others are made by the manager, but with input and consultation.

3. They depend less on positional than on personal power.

4. They know when and how to make personal policy exceptions, without causing a team riot.

5. They are thoughtful when matching individuals to a team, or matching a team or individual to an assignment.

6. They balance concern for tasks and concern for people. They are neither slave drivers nor country club managers.

7. They understand the elements of trust and work to gain it from their employees. They are perceived as fair, inclusive, good communicators, and competent in their own right.[7]

While some sources anticipate that this will be the next generation of workaholics, I don't agree. According to Mercer Human Resources Consulting, 64 percent of Baby Boom Echo employees reported reaching a balance between home and work. Only about 40 percent of the other generations reported finding such a balance. In addition, other trends, such as spirituality in the workplace, are at play that will continue to reinforce balance as a priority.

At the same time, however, this generation is not afraid of hard work. They will be more efficient, working smarter instead of longer. A 2001 study found that 88 percent of the Echos surveyed had specific goals for the next five years and were confident about reaching them.[8] This type of goal-oriented optimism would not be expected from either Boomers or Xers. Echos reflect their parents' priority around education. Not only are they well educated in the traditional sense, but also most hit the workforce with relevant work experience or internships to their credit. In addition, Echos are expected to continue their education throughout adulthood, consistently seeking out job-related and other types of training.

What Echos Want

While companies are eager for the hard-working Echos to join the workforce, they will find that this generation has strong demands for their employers—demands that they will expect to be met. In their book *Managing Generation Y*, Bruce Tulgan and Carolyn A. Martin cite Echo expectations of the workplace including: challenging work that matters, clearly delegated assignments balanced with freedom and flexibility, increased responsibility as a reward for accomplishment, ongoing training/learning opportunities, and mentor relationships. In another book, *Generations*, authors William Strauss and Neil Howe predict that the Baby Boom Echos, who are also expected to become politically active, will require even more dramatic employment adjustments, such as:

- ❏ Pay equity among all workers
- ❏ Fewer job definitions
- ❏ A reestablished middle class
- ❏ Downgraded salaries for CEOs and other executives
- ❏ Trade barriers
- ❏ Government regulation of labor standards
- ❏ Revitalized unions [9]

Not only demanding, the Echos may also be needy and harder to please. They are expected to require more direction and supervision than the Boomers or Xers. Companies will need strong team leaders to manage them. Training, orientation, and consistent feedback will also be important to their success. A majority (67 percent) expressed an interest in the opportunity to take time away for training—compared to 52 percent or less for the other generations. Echos also reported being less satisfied at work—significantly less satisfied than the other generations—with both their job and their companies. Less than half of Echos said they feel fairly treated at work, compared to 64 percent of all generations. In addition, while 75 percent of Xers feel that they are being challenged with interesting work, only 64 percent of Echos do. One reason for this may be that they feel they are ready to move to the next rung of the corporate ladder, but haven't yet done so.[10]

Company loyalty and motivation of the Baby Boom Echos is influenced by factors other than pay, especially when compared to the other generations. As mentioned above, Echos are very loyal to their managers, whom they view as caring coaches. When asked about factors that affect their commitment and motivation to work, 82 percent cited flexible working arrangements, a figure much higher than that for the other generations. While the other generations most often cited base pay as the primary work factor, fewer Echos did. Still, more than half of the Echos said they would be willing to leave their current employer for another offering better benefits.

THE MILLENNIUM GENERATION: BORN SINCE 2000

As I mentioned in the thumbnail sketches of the generations at the beginning of this chapter, I am breaking out a fifth, new generation that I call The Millennium Generation, or the Millennials, to describe babies being born since the turn of the 21st century.* As interesting as all this generational information is, it is only part of the picture. New babies are being born every day, and historical, political, and even entertainment events will influence them in ways that I cannot even dare to imagine. With my futurist hat firmly in place, I see young people entering the work place who will be comfortable with diversity, who will expect equal pay as an everyday

*Many writers use the term *millennials* to refer to people born in the 1980s and 1990s. Again, terminology can be confusing. I prefer my usage; it was, after all, in 2000 that we celebrated the "millennium."

occurrence, and who will be flexible and interested in carving out their own niche both at home and at work. Technology will be so advanced that the time-clock-punching mentality will be a thing of the past. Results will rule. Recognition and reward will follow naturally and without angst or struggle.

One thing is for sure. Millennials will live a long time. By 2020, we may have five generations working side by side. Surveys and studies will continue to pour out of established and prestigious sources as each generation enters each phase of their lives. Companies will have instant access to all of this information. More importantly, though, companies will have a front-row seat for the interactions, associations, and priorities of the four or five generations working side by side. This first hand information will prove the most valuable in determining how to best manage the generations for maximum employee satisfaction and productivity.

MANY GENERATIONS: ONE WORKFORCE

Insight into the differences among the generations is beneficial to employers seeking to create a workplace where people can do their best work. Generalizations aside, every one in every generation is a person. At the end of the day, each individual wants to be recognized as such: an individual, not a number or statistic or label. This is not preaching, this is priority insight #1.

What generation are you in? As I already mentioned, I am considered a Baby Boomer. In researching the generations, I found characteristics I shared with my Boomer brethren, and ones I did not. No big surprise! I bet you would say the same thing. More importantly, though, I found a common thread throughout all of the generations—as individuals, regardless of their age, they share a desire for individual dignity. In the workplace this translates into:

- ❏ Respect
- ❏ Fair treatment
- ❏ Equality
- ❏ Balance
- ❏ Flexibility
- ❏ Appropriate feedback
- ❏ Job enhancement and advancement opportunities

GENERATIONAL DIVERSITY

First off, it's inevitable that the generations will all be present in the work-force at the same time. Smart businesses, however, will proactively seek generational diversity in their employee base for a number of reasons, including:

- ❑ *Wisdom and Experience*: A new appreciation for the corporate wisdom, but also the life wisdom, of the older worker is renewing their role as a valuable asset.

- ❑ *Fresh Ideas and Fearlessness*: Younger workers bring a value in their "why not" ways that have come as a result of their fresh approach and independence.

- ❑ *Individual Wisdom and Skills*: Regardless of their age, each individual brings a unique skill and experience set. Finding just the right blend for a given position requires that we open up opportunities across the generations and reach out for the diverse and wonderful things they each can offer.

- ❑ *The Need for More Workers*: Many sources predict worker shortages in the millions in the first half of the 21st century.

- ❑ *Reflection of the Marketplace*: All these vital and active generations will be the vital and active marketplace from which your customers will come. An employee base that mirrors the marketplace is largely accepted and expected to be more effective.

CONCLUSION

What we are seeing today, early in the 21st century, is just the tip of the iceberg. We can find examples of four generations active in the workplace scattered here and there. At this point, they are novel enough even to be newsworthy. By 2050, though, four or even five generations will be working together in full force. It won't just be Seniors working at Burger King or serving as ex-officio board members, and it won't just be young people, still wet behind the ears, needing to learn to fit in and earn their stripes. Many generations of workers—all strong, all valuable, and all side-by-side—will provide unprecedented opportunities for development and profitability. Combining the wisdom and experience of the older worker with the energy and stamina of the young, the workplace of the future stands to gain considerably.

Finding and keeping the best and the brightest from all the generations will be the challenge of the future. Management, compensation, scheduling, and training will all be affected by the multigenerational workforce. These will be the challenges covered in the second half of the book.

NOTES

1. Ron Zemke, Claire Raines, and Bob Filipczak, *Generations at Work: Managing the Clash of Veterans, Boomers, Xers, and Nexters in Your Workplace* (New York: AMACOM, 2000).

2. Alison Stein Wellner, "Generational Divide," *American Demographics,* October 2000, pp. 52–56, 58.

3. Edie Weiner, interview, August 2003.

4. Quoted in Wellner, "Generational Divide, p. 545.

5. Robin Toner, "Trust In the Military Heightens Among Baby Boomers' Children," *The New York Times,* May 27, 2003, p. A1.

6. Eric Hazard, "Mercer (HR Consulting): Gen Y Positive About Career But Not Satisfied," *www.PlanSponsor.com,* July 16, 2003.

7. Zemke, Raines, and Filipczak, *Generations at Work.*

8. Ibid, p. 144.

9. William Strauss and Neil Howe, *Generations: The History of America's Future, 1584 to 2069* (New York: William Morrow, 1992).

10. Hazard, "Mercer (HR Consulting): Gen Y Positive About Career."

CHAPTER 4

TREND 4: DIVERSITY

AMERICA THE COLORFUL

My husband is of English and Dutch descent. His ancestors came to this country at the time of the Mayflower. According to him, it was *on* the Mayflower but who knows—he was raised on a farm in upstate New York. Although his family has been in America for many generations, we still took a trip to Holland to trace his roots. Being as American as possible, all the way back to the Mayflower after all, he is still interested in discovering and connecting to his roots beyond American shores. In addition, he was brought up Baptist and became a Baptist minister, following in the footsteps of his grandfather.

I am a second generation American. My grandparents came to America through Ellis Island by way of Russia, Poland, and Austria. They had thick foreign accents and spoke a mixture of English and Yiddish. They escaped the pogroms in Russia and were thrilled to be in America. I was raised in the small, tight-knit world of a Jewish enclave until I entered high school. The larger world outside opened to me when I attended a city high school and large college.

Then came our daughter. What a wonderful combination she is. Lindsay is a mix of the best of Christianity and Judaism. Her best friend is a Nigerian girl she met in first grade. Somewhere around fifth grade, after years of constant companionship, Lindsay mentioned that she and her best friend were somewhat different. Her comment was, "When I went to church with Nneka's family, I noticed for the first time that I was a different color and wondered if Nneka ever feels different when she is with our family."

The girls suddenly began talking about the fact that one was light-skinned and the other dark. To them, it was a mildly interesting point of reference, but not something that should keep them apart or mark them as different from one another. Through e-mail and visits, they have stayed best friends through college. Now twenty-one, they are part of a new generation that is refreshingly unconcerned about "differences" that drove people apart in the not-too-distant past. Their generation also seems to care very deeply about the future of our world.

Last summer, the girls were sharing photos from college: Nneka proudly showing off her six-foot tall Caucasian boyfriend, Lindsay doing the same with her African-American date for the big dance. I asked the girls if they noticed anything unusual in the pictures.

"No," they shrugged. "Why?"

If only all of us could be this color-blind, this accepting of mixtures, this indifferent to differences, because this is the undeniable future of the American population—full of mixtures and differences. "They have no prejudice because they have no fear," believes Natalie Allen, president of Philadelphia Academies and my good friend. Philadelphia Academies is a not-for-profit organization that links companies with public schools to help at-risk high school students succeed and graduate. She has worked with urban high school students for twenty years and sees firsthand how fear is the root cause of prejudice. "The earlier we can form bonds that have nothing to do with what color you are or where you are from, the more balance our work places will have in the future," she says. "Respecting and embracing differences, not fearing them, will enable us to create the best work environment."

This chapter covers the broad topic of diversity. Gender, race, religion, creed, disability, sexual preference, and nationality shape who we are and how we perceive the world. They influence us as much as the historical factors that define our generations. The diversity of the emerging workforce creates both challenges and opportunities for employers.

IMMIGRATION AND DIVERSITY

Diversity in America is hugely affected by immigration. Worldwide, more than 150 million people live in a country different from their birthplace;

more than a quarter of these people chose to live in the United States. By 2050, our population is expected to grow by 129 million and of this number 75 million are expected to be immigrants.[1] Traditionally, immigrants to the United States came from Western and Central Europe. Irish, English, Germans, and Italians flooded Ellis Island in pursuit of the American dream. While they came with their own languages, cultures, and traditions, they had, by and large, one key thing in common: They were more or less "white."

More recently, that has not been the case. Since the 1965 Immigration Act lifted restrictions on immigration from non-Christian countries, America has seen an influx of immigrants representing many more races and creeds, and until recently, the number of white immigrants has steadily declined. In 1970, 62 percent of foreign-born U.S. residents were of European and non-Hispanic descent. By 1997, this figure had dropped to just 17 percent, a percentage that has held steady since. More white immigrants have been coming to the United States recently from Eastern Europe, Africa, the former Soviet Union, and even Canada. The article cites U.S. Immigration of Naturalization Service (INS) reports that say ten times more white immigrants came to America from the Soviet Union during the 1990s than came during the 1980s. From 1997 to 2000, the share of the total foreign-born U.S. residents who were white and from Africa increased from 30 percent to 38 percent. During the same period, the share of foreign-born black residents from Africa decreased by 10 percent.[2]

CORPORATE DIVERSITY = CORPORATE REALITY

America has always been a melting pot and it still is. From 1996 to 2002, 27 percent of all international immigrants came to the United States.[3] This, I believe, will not change in the future. What will change, however, are the colors that mix in the melting pot. If the shades in the melting pot of the past came from a box of eight colors, the shades of the future will come from a box of sixty-four. What will change, too, are the demands upon companies to reflect this increasingly broad range of shades.

There are two reasons that the demands upon companies will increase vis-à-vis diversity. The first and most obvious reason reflects the legal requirements placed upon businesses in the name of diversity. In the view of

Marc Silbert, a specialist in ERISA law, diversity is one area where the law is ahead of reality. Many laws governing diversity date back to the 1960s, and we are still trying to catch up—to make diversity a reality in our work-force. The second reason is that an even more powerful force will make diversity inevitable. The labor pool itself is becoming so blended, so "color-ful," that employers of the future, simply by filling their ranks, will be hiring a more diverse workforce. Quite simply, there will be no way to avoid it.

DEFINING DIVERSITY

Diversity has been a corporate buzzword for years. An Internet search for the key word "diversity" revealed nearly 400,000 matches. More telling, a search of book titles on the subject of "diversity in the workplace" resulted in more than 200 matches.

According to *Webster's Dictionary* online, diversity is a noun meaning "the condition of being different or diverse; variety." In the workforce, di-versity can be defined as differences among employees. Under Title VII of the Civil Rights Act of 1964, these differences specifically include national origin, race, color, religion, and gender. Under various other state and fed-eral laws, specified employee differences include age (40+ years), sexual orientation, and disability. I will call this "Definition 1." For me, there are other definitions of diversity that go beyond simple and obvious attributes. The second definition of diversity is a labor pool so colorful and blended that it is nearly impossible not to see its reflection in your employees. Fi-nally, in "Definition 3," diversity is acceptance and respect for individual differences. This definition focuses on inclusion rather than exclusion and makes the story of Nneka and Lindsay the current norm rather than the unusual exception.

DIVERSITY DEFINITION 1: THE WORKFORCE AS A COLLECTION OF DIFFERENT PEOPLES

Under the first definition of diversity, specific and obvious differences among workers (often defined by law) reveal at a glance the rapidly growing variety of people who come together in the workplace. The workforce can be seen as a collection of different peoples working together toward common goals, yet each bringing his or her own perspective and abilities. Let's look at some of these differences.

RACE AND ETHNICITY

As America continues to be the land of opportunity, the makeup of the workforce continues to change dramatically. Minority groups are growing at an unprecedented rate, especially Asian-Americans and Hispanics. According to the U.S. Census Bureau, for the first time since the early 1930s, one of every ten Americans is foreign-born, due mainly to explosive growth in the Hispanic population.

As shown in Figure 4-1, by the year 2050, U.S. Census Bureau projects the following racial/ethnic distribution: 55 percent White, 21 percent Hispanic, 14 percent Black, 9 percent Asian, and 1 percent American Indian.[4]

Asian-Americans, are the fastest growing ethnic group, multiplying ten-fold from about one million in 1970 to nearly 11 million by 2000.[5] By 2050, the number of Asian Americans is expected to double and make up about 10 percent of the population.[6]

The huge growth of the Hispanic population, however, has had the

Figure 4-1. Racial/ethnic distribution of United States in 2050.

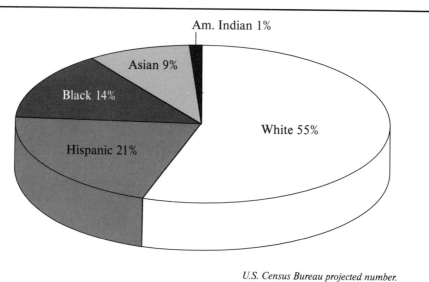

U.S. Census Bureau projected number.

greatest impact on the diversity of the America. Data from the 2000 Census shows a 60 percent growth in the Hispanic population in the United States in the last ten years, making it now the largest minority. The Census found 35.3 million Hispanic residents in America compared with 22.4 million in 1990. This was roughly 3 million higher than previous estimates from the Census Bureau, a difference attributed by demographers to the rising number of illegal immigrants.[7] By 2050, the total number of U.S. residents of Hispanic descent is expected to reach 98 million.[8] By comparison, the 2000 Census reported that number of Blacks rose to 34.7 million from 30 million in 1990, an increase of only 16 percent.

Clearly, this evolution in the racial and ethnic composition of our population will have an impact on the workforce of the future. Every human resource function, from recruiting through communication, will need to serve a mixed population. One set of benefits won't fit all, one type of training won't fit all, and one language may not even fit all. Companies will need to understand the mix—cultures, similarities and differences, communication styles, training needs—you name it. Then, beyond understanding the mix, they will need to accept, accommodate, and attract this mix.

Perpetuating Problems: Illegal Immigration

In 2001, there were six million illegal immigrants in the United States. These illegal aliens come primarily from Mexico, where a worker typically makes one-tenth of the amount earned working in the United States. Some believe this poses a threat to the legitimate labor pool of the United States, since the number of illegal aliens represents 3.5 percent of the work force. Compare this figure to the current unemployment rate of 6.1 percent(according to the Department of Labor as of September 9, 2003), and you get a sense of the "opportunity lost" for American workers. The counter-point, however, is that most of the jobs held by these illegal aliens are low-paying, cash-under-the-table, no-benefits, manual-labor jobs that few American workers would want. The real problem, then, is that the continued practice of hiring illegal immigrants perpetuates the worst kind of employment: workplaces where there is no acceptance or respect, and no enlightenment, just cheap labor.

RELIGION

The *Encyclopedia of American Religions,* 7th edition, cites more than 2,000 religious organizations in the United States.[9] While Christianity is still the largest religion in America, the number of Jews, Hindus, Muslims, and Buddhists continues to grow.

In an interesting new twist, a 2001 study sponsored by four American Islamic organizations estimated that there were between six and seven million Muslims in the United States, and that the number of mosques had increased by 25 percent in six years, to about 1,200. If the study is accurate, it would indicate that there are now more Muslims than Jews in the United States, since the commonly accepted number of American Jews is six million.[10]

I will convey more information about religion in the next chapter, Trend 5: Trust, Respect, and Ethics. From a diversity standpoint, though, it is important to acknowledge that many religions continue to grow within the United States, and they will contribute to the increasing diversity of our nation's workforce. While individual accommodation may be impossible, employers should be aware of and tuned into this religious diversity.

GEOGRAPHIC DISPERSION

The United States is not universally diverse. As people have immigrated here, they have not settled evenly across the country. For example, among all immigrants to the United States between 1996 and 2002, 25 percent went to California. As a result, California is the most diverse state in the union. By 2025, an estimated 34 percent of California residents will be white. In comparison, Maine, the least diverse state, is expected to be more than 97 percent white in 2025.[11] It is interesting to note, however, that even in racially homogeneous Maine, the Lewiston-Auburn area of the state has seen an influx of immigrants from Somalia since the late 1990s, which has caused some controversy. In addition, there has been an increase in Hispanic migrant workers drawn to jobs in the blueberry and potato industries in areas farther north in Maine. In the order shown, Los Angeles, New York City, San Francisco, Miami, and Chicago are the major American cities with the most foreign-born residents.[12]

As in the case of the Somalis who have settled in Lewiston, Maine, different ethnic and religious groups have tended to congregate in certain geographies. Historically, the Hispanic population has concentrated in the Southwest, California, Florida, and New York. Since the late 1990s, Mexican and Central American immigrants have begun to settle in North Carolina, Georgia, and Iowa, where previously a Hispanic population was nearly nonexistent.[13] An October 2000 article in *The Economist* stated that Arab Americans are mostly concentrated in the industrial states of Pennsylvania, New Jersey, Ohio, Illinois, and Michigan. The article went on to say that the city of Detroit, with an Arab American population of 300,000 in 2000, is home to the largest concentration of Arabs anywhere in the world outside of the Middle East.[14] Since the 1965 Immigration Act lifted restrictions on immigrants from "non-Christian" countries, new immigrant religious groups have tended to settle in the states of California and Minnesota, and in the cities of New York, Philadelphia, and Chicago.

GENDER: THE ISSUE THAT WON'T GO AWAY

You would think that gender as a workplace diversity issue should be a thing of the past. Men and women have been working together in fairly equal numbers for more than forty years. Women have entered traditionally male-oriented jobs (and vice versa). More and more women are supervising men than ever before. Still, gender just seems to be one of those issues that never really goes away. Unfortunately, many of the same problems that have plagued women in the workplace for decades are still prevalent today.

Unequal Pay

First, the bad news. The wage gap isn't just still around, it is actually getting wider. A Congressional study released in January 2002 found that "full-time female managers earned on average less than their male counterparts in the ten industries that employ more than 70 percent of all female workers, and in seven of the ten fields, the pay difference widened between 1995 and 2000."[15]

The pay gap can be attributed partially to motherhood. Working women do relatively well up through their early thirties. Then, just as they hit their stride in their career and enter management positions, they also are having children. As a result, they often pull back on their careers—taking leaves of absence, going part-time, or at a minimum, seeking better work-life balance. According to an article in *The Washington Post National Weekly,* 60 percent of female managers are not currently raising children, compared to 40 percent of male managers. It appears that women who wish to be managers are faced with the choice between delaying having children for the sake of their careers or delaying their careers for the sake of having children.

Different Career Tracks

Once the children are grown, however, it's a whole new ball game. This phenomenon leads to a very intriguing issue regarding women, men, and aging. For the first time, we see husbands retiring at exactly the same time that their wives are reaching the highest point in their careers. The last thing these women want to do is to retire and play golf with their husband. This can create tensions within households that may contribute to rising divorce rates in the older age groups.

There are millions of women over age 50 who are expected to join and stay in the workforce over the next ten years—truly a new precedent. Major growth is expected in the number of women over age 50 who occupy professional managerial or technical jobs. That market is expected to expand to over 10 million women. In almost one third of all married households, the wife now outearns the husband. This is creating a major subculture of older, affluent, working women with dependent spouses.

Promotions and Senior Positions

While there seems to be a general sentiment that women in business are doing better than ever, that is not necessarily true. It is not just the widening wage gap, it is also the issue of promotions and senior positions. While women hold twice as many senior management jobs as they did in 1955, most are still outsiders. Women make up less than 16 percent of the executive ranks. The "good old boys" network still exists—90 percent of senior line managers in Fortune 500 companies are men.[16] While the majority of white male executives talk a good game and put on a good face for gender balance, the truth lies behind the closed doors of "boys clubs" where they feel the *real* work gets done.

"Not a whole lot has changed," states Molly D. Shepard, president and CEO of The Leader's Edge, LLC.[17] Shepard has more than twenty years' experience in career counseling, leadership development, executive coaching, and executive search. Prior to founding The Leader's Edge, she was chairman, president, and co-founder of Manchester, Inc., one of the world's largest career development consulting firms. Shepard started The Leaders Edge as a resource for executive women. She sees that men are questioning women hard—questioning their commitment, questioning their loyalty.

According to Shepard, women are leaving corporate America at twice the rate of men. However, they are not leaving the workforce entirely: They are either starting their own businesses, or looking for a more inclusive corporate culture. It's interesting to note that while the three heralded female whistleblowers of 2002—Cynthia Cooper of Worldcom, Colleen Rowley of the FBI, and Sherron Watkins of Enron—were so widely hailed by the media, they posed a real threat to the status quo of business. One can only imagine what names those gutsy women were called at the upper echelons of their organizations.

Should the Government Step In?

Some say the problem is that the U.S. government is not pushing the business community for an increased number of executive women. To date, all the pressure has had to come from other outside sources. Perhaps we need to follow the example of the Norwegian government, which has announced that it is prepared to take action to force the election of more women to boards, setting a goal of 40 percent by 2005. As of July 2003, women were represented on only 8.4 percent of corporate boards in Norway. In the United States, women don't fare much better. They held only 12.4 percent of board seats of the Fortune 1000 companies in 2001.[18]

Shepard sees the trend toward smaller boards of directors as a deterrent to the increased membership of women on the boards. She believes that at least two women need to be on any given executive committee or board of directors. "One woman on a board will most often be ignored or forced to conform to the 'male' norm," she says. "It's when you have at least two or more women in the room—that's when you see the dynamic begin to shift, and when women can get their voices and ideas heard."[19] Her goal is for women to comprise 20 percent of board and senior executive positions—a figure that today stands at around 10 percent, depending on your source. In Shepard's world, these executive women will be able to hold these positions and still maintain a balance between work and family. She believes it is possible and, in fact, will make for better, more enlightened business, but it can't exist in the corporate norm of today. "Today's 24/7 business world makes it impossible for anyone to find work/life balance, not just women," comments Shepard. "The difference is that women are less likely to define themselves by their job. I'm seeing more and more women leaving their big deal corporate jobs in order to find a better balance between work and family, either in a new company or by starting their own businesses."

Women Who Don't Want What Men Have

I saw a speech by John Boscia, CEO of Lincoln Financial, who told this story: He asked two highly qualified women to be chief executive officers of large subsidiaries of Lincoln, and both women declined due to work/balance issues. This is a relatively new phenomenon, but one well worth the attention of enlightened employers. Women are no longer willing to give it all up to succeed in a man's world. Instead, they are seeking to change the world to allow both business success and balance in their private lives. According to Judith Rodin, the first woman to be president of an Ivy League school, the University of Pennsylvania, "Women following us say 'I look at you and I don't want to be you.'" This is both a challenge and an opportunity for businesses in the future. In the long run, these female issues of work/life balance and priorities other than career will be of great benefit to companies.

In early 2004, I saw Karen Hughes, a White House counselor, interviewed by Barbara Walters on *20/20*. Hughes was promoting President George W. Bush, her book, and the fact that moving her family back to Texas from Washington, D.C. was a wise choice for her. She made a life decision to benefit her family, yet she stays undeniably powerful. She is talking to the White House every day, traveling, and contributing, all while better meeting the needs of her family.

Change Is in the Air

There is reason for hope, however, so let's move on to the good news.

Eighty-three percent of U.S. jobs are now categorized as service-providing. The majority of these jobs rely on diligent, low-ego, cooperative, traditionally female skills, according to *U.S. News and World Report*.[20] At the same time, the traditionally male spatial and mathematical skills, required of service-providing technical jobs, are becoming less and less male dominated. Girls are improving in mathematics and technical areas of study, and are becoming increasingly dominant in student government, academic performance, and extracurricular activities.

The gender gap has been traced to an expectation gap, and today the expectations of girls are soaring, while for boys they are plummeting. There seems to be a feeling among some that today's elementary school boys today are, shall we say, a payback generation—the one that has to compensate for the advantages given to males in the past.[21] These are the Millennials that will be hitting the work force in the next twenty years.

Natalie Allen of Philadelphia Academies sees the growing power of the female first-hand, everyday. Working with inner-city youth since 1988, she has seen the inner strength and determination that fuel girls today. She adds, "Girls today have several strong female role models in business. Those of us who have struggled and fought to attain an executive position and still be an involved and caring wife and mother are setting the stage for the next generation."[22] Celebrating the women who achieve and spreading the word about them is making a difference for the outlook, expectations, and self-confidence of young women across the country.

Mars and Venus at Work

Common ground needs to be found for effective communication between men and women in the workplace. Molly D. Shepard has researched the many differences between men and women in business settings. For example, she finds that women are more intuitive, ask more questions, and delve deeper into the issues. In addition, she notes, women nod to communicate understanding, not necessarily agreement. Men nod to agree. So we have male managers and coworkers talking on and on, assuming that their female employees and coworkers are nodding in agreement, when that may not be the case at all. Moreover, men tend to listen passively without expression, offering little or no acknowledgement of what they are hearing. This often leads women to repeat the same point over and over seeking consent and unsure if the men have actually heard them. It is helpful to understand this. Watch for this behavior in your next meeting.

The genders also differ in their negotiation style. Quite simply, women traditionally don't negotiate and men do. Women are more likely to expect that the offer they are being given is the best and most fair available. Men are more likely to ask for more. Also, women are less willing to give up personal balance for the sake of the job, whereas men are traditionally more job-centered. Often, this leads to men viewing women as less committed and/or less able to perform job duties, though that is rarely the case. In fact, as I explain in Chapter 5, the workforce of the future will seek better work/ life balance regardless of age or gender. A woman's approach, particularly in executive management, could be a strong aid in successfully creating this balance.

Women also view power and define success differently from men. Men tend to see power as authority; women tend to view it as influence. Men view their success primarily as a function of their career. For women, success may be a function of any, or all, of several factors, including but not limited to career. Women may find success through their jobs, their marriages, their children, their volunteer work, or their friendships. In short, women perceive success as a choice they make. For men, success equals job; there's no choice about it.

Let me be sure to make the point that these are norms that have been studied. We all know exceptions. It is the variety that keeps the workplace interesting.

Sexual Preference

Same-sex couples now account for one in nine of the 594,000 live-in, non-officially married households. Even though gay and lesbian couples are adopting and having children in growing numbers, they are, by and large, a group with a great deal of disposable income. Remember the DINKs of the 1980s? DINK stood for Dual Income No Kids, and they were the retail darlings of their day—childless couples with nothing but time and money to spend on themselves. In the new millennium, gay and lesbian couples are the new DINKs. This status makes them very attractive to employers, as well as to marketers. These couples are buying above-average-priced housing and cars, plus are spending extensively on travel and leisure items. Retailers are targeting the gay market with special promotions and "gay only" tours. Niche magazines directed to this market are increasingly popular.

The Gay Index

There seems to be another reason for employers to "go where the gays are." Richard Florida, from the Software Industry Center at Carnegie Mellon University, cites a "gay index," meaning the percentage of gays in a city, as a reliable index for the attractiveness of a market. Florida says that a high percentage of gay and lesbian residents indicates an area of increased tolerance and openness to diversity, with many amenities that attract the best workers. These amenities are things like cultural and arts venues, good restaurants, and a "happening" social scene.[23]

DISABILITY

I recently attended a lecture by the CEO of eBay, Meg Whitman. She shared a touching story about a letter she received asking her to meet with one of her primary vendors. We all know the eBay story of success. There are 150,000 vendors, many of whom make their living auctioning their wares on eBay. Much to Whitman's surprise, the vendor she was to meet at a vendor conference in Texas was a young adult male with cerebral palsy. He and his parents wanted to meet and thank her, not so much for the opportunity to make a living on eBay, but rather because through eBay, he was not disabled. The mother and father have both quit their other jobs to work with their son's successful enterprise.

We are all familiar with the Americans with Disabilities Act. Many individuals with, for example, Down's syndrome work successfully if they are placed in jobs that are a good match for their skills, abilities, and interests, and which give them appropriate levels of support. For the most part, though, handicapped workers are employed in specialized environments through organizations such as Goodwill Industries. In the future, however, this may change. Many more young children with disabilities are being "mainstreamed" through the public schools. Supported with a series of professionals and full-time aides, customized plans, and government funding, children with mild to fairly severe handicaps are moving through school, grade by grade, alongside children their own age.

The number of children with special needs in schools is increasing. Seventeen percent of American children, almost 12 million, suffer from learning, developmental, and/or behavioral disorders. Every few years since 1971, the number of children taking Ritalin for Attention Deficit Hyperactivity Disorder (ADHD) has doubled. Autism is increasing. Up to 10 percent of public school children have learning disabilities. In California alone, the number of children in special education programs because of learning disabilities rose 200 percent from 1987 to 1998.[24] Finding ways to tap into this potential work force, matching skills with needs will be a great step forward in staffing our companies.

DIVERSITY DEFINITION 2: THE WORKFORCE IN A BLENDER

All of the "Definition 1" statistics point to a workforce that will reflect the "box of 64 colors" in the future. If for no other reason than that it would cost too much to find, pay, and keep a single "like-me" type of employee in the future, employees will become an ever more diverse group. In short, the company of the future will not be able to avoid hiring a wide variety of people.

Definition 2 describes what will happen as first generation immigrants become second- and third-generation immigrants. They inter-marry. They have children. They combine and assimilate cultures, traditions, and values. I did. My daughter did even more so. We are all part of the workforce in a blender.

In the spirit of history repeating itself, this has happened in our country before. In the early 1900s, when all those Eastern Europeans greeted Lady Liberty, they came and stayed in pockets. There were Italians, Polish, Irish, and Germans. They lived with "their own" in neighborhoods where their culture, language, foods, and traditions could largely remain the same.

English was often a foreign language. There were clashes, fights, and put-downs among the various groups.

The roots of these neighborhoods still exist: the Italian Market in Philadelphia still celebrates its annual Italian festival with pole climbing and greased pigs, and the Germantown section in Columbus, Ohio still boasts of the best potato salad and Bratwurst anywhere. Now, though, the offspring of those early immigrants are not so much Italian or Dutch or German or Polish as they are American. They ventured out from their enclosed ethnic pockets. The children begin to interact on the ball fields, in the schoolyards, and at the local dances. Dutch women married Irish men; German men married Italian women. Even the traditions we learned from our ancestors were frozen in time, while the countries they came from moved on and developed new traditions, sometimes losing the old ones in the process. I have a friend who went to Poland and was shocked that they did not dance the polka!

The fact that my husband is of English and Dutch descent or that I am of Russian Jewish heritage makes for an interesting story, but it no longer actively shapes who we are, where we live, or how we choose our friends.

This is where our nation is heading once again. The groups may have changed; the story is the same. In another fifty years, it won't matter if your grandmother's grandmother came from Puerto Rico or Africa, Germany or Ireland, you will just be American. Remembering heritage is important; having prejudice because of it does not make sense.

Some Multiracial Facts and Figures

The 2000 Census indicates that the number of multiracial residents is growing and that, generally, they are young. About one in twenty residents of the 1.8 million who checked that they are black also checked at least one other race in the Census. This is particularly true for those under eighteen years old. By 2050, 21 percent of Americans are expected to claim mixed ethnicity.[25] Almost 6 million Baby Boomers declare themselves to be multiracial or "other."

Married couples are increasingly blended as well—6 percent are of different races and 12 percent are of mixed races. In California, there is a growing blend of American and Hispanics: Third-generation Hispanics marry non-Hispanics more than 50 percent of the time.[26] Also, according to the Census, 30 percent of the multiracial population is concentrated in five states: New York, Texas, Florida, Hawaii, and Illinois.

One interesting reflection of this multiracial trend is its growing prevalence in advertising. Models of mixed race are growing in popularity, particularly in advertising that targets the younger, "hip" market, such as Calvin Klein, Gap, and Mitsubishi.

THE BLENDED WORKFORCE IS A GOOD THING

In his book, *The Global Me: New Cosmopolitans and the Competitive Edge: Picking Globalisms Winners and Losers*, G. Pascal Zachary expresses his positive views about the blending population.[27] He sees the mixing of races, ethnic groups, and nationalities happening at unprecedented levels that are only just beginning. He calls these blended citizens of the future "mongrels" and "hybrids"—not the words I would choose. I agree, however, with his views. These blends of people will have a positive impact on the places where they live and work. They tend to be more inclusive and fair-minded, flexible, and open, making them attractive to employers.

The point is that the labor pool is becoming less and less of a menu where companies can hire one from Column A and one from Column B to fill predetermined quotas. Incidentally, this is why I believe that hiring quotas are obsolete. Quota hiring served a purpose. It opened corporate eyes to other possibilities to which they were previously blind. By legal force, it jump-started the process of hiring someone different. Going forward, however, affirmative action quotas will not be enough. For one thing, the workforce in a blender makes it too easy. (I can't help but recall a certain unenlightened manager I once knew who exclaimed "If I can hire one candidate who's a half-black, half-Hispanic female, I'll have finished my quota for the year!") As Natalie Allen puts it, "Diversity is not something we can put on our agenda, accomplish by December, and move on."[28]

Diversity in the future will be evolutionary, not revolutionary. It will have more to do with acceptance, flexibility, and respect. It will be about hiring someone different because it will broaden our perspective, open up new views, and better reflect our markets, not because it will get us a check mark in the affirmative action box on a review form. My daughter Lindsay and her close friend Nneka are the true harbingers of the future—where diversity is a non-issue.

DIVERSITY DEFINITION 3: A WORKFORCE OF ACCEPTANCE AND RESPECT

The third definition of diversity is necessary to drive home the point that just hiring a diverse group of employees will not be enough. Acceptance and respect of the differences among employees will also be key. Often I see diversity linked to the term tolerance. I am not a big fan of this association. I view tolerance as similar to hiring quotas—a concept that once served a purpose that is now becoming obsolete. In the workforce of the future, employers will not merely tolerate differences among employees; they will embrace them. The diversity of their workforces will make companies stronger in every area, and employers who recognize this fact today will have a leg up on future success.

THE DIVERSITY CONTINUUM

Diversity is a phenomenon that is moving along a continuum. Initially, when people all strived for the comfort of sameness, variety was a threat. So at one end, diversity was cause for *segregation*. Then, thanks to inspirational leaders such as Dr. Martin Luther King, Jr., we slowly moved toward *tolerance*. People didn't necessarily change their views. We just learned to "put up and shut up" about things and other people that were different. The next stage along the continuum is *acceptance*, which not only recognizes and tolerates differences, but also respects and welcomes them. The other end of the continuum *celebrates* diversity. As illustrated in Figure 4-2, diversity challenges us to move from segregation, through tolerance, then acceptance, to celebration.

Figure 4-2. The Diversity Continuum.

| SEGREGATE | TOLERATE | ACCEPT | CELEBRATE |

Different people and companies are at different points on the continuum. Radical groups like white supremacists define themselves by their hateful segregation—actively refusing even to tolerate differences. Then there are those like Oprah Winfrey and Jimmy Carter, who embrace differences among people and welcome those who are different with open arms.

In addition, people are generally at different places on the continuum relative to different groups. Where we are on the continuum at any given time with regard to a particular group is shaped by any number of factors, such as where we live, how we were reared, and what is happening in the world. Certainly the September 11, 2001, terrorist attacks on America are a dramatic example of this. In the United States, anyone of Arab descent became immediately suspect, and many Americans slid instantly from acceptance to fear of anyone who even looked Middle Eastern.

WHERE COMPANIES ARE ON THE CONTINUUM

Most of corporate America is somewhere around "tolerate." Whether closer to "putting up with" or closer to "acceptance" varies according to influencers such as company size, location, or industry. By and large, a company moves further and faster along the continuum toward acceptance when: 1) it is forced to, or 2) its leaders accept and encourage diversity. For example, companies become more accepting of diversity either when they are located where the population is more diverse, or when they operate in an industry whose employment needs can be met only by accepting diverse employees. Geography is an obvious factor. A company hiring from the labor pool in California, the most diverse state in the country, sees people of all backgrounds when interviewing for a position. In Maine, however, the opposite is the case.

Industry also plays an important role. In some industries, the need for employees with specialized skills is so great that employers, eager to find enough employees, have been forced to reach out to a more diverse labor pool. For example, the dramatic shortage of nurses in the United States (and worldwide) has led to a major exodus of qualified workers from poorer nations to wealthier ones. Thousands of nurses have left South Africa, Ghana, Jamaica, Trinidad and Tobago to come and work in the United States and other more developed countries.[29]

Yet another example is the dearth of high-tech professionals. Congress has authorized an increase in H-1B visas for highly skilled international workers. At the same time, many American companies have moved various technical functions to other nations. Intel has a chip-processing plant in Costa Rica, and AOL/Time Warner is building a global customer service center in the Philippines. China, with more college students graduating than ever before, is becoming a ripe resource for global research and development.[30]

Teachers are also increasingly diverse. According to an article in *U.S. News & World Report*, school districts are recruiting teachers from other nations. Cities such as Salt Lake City and Philadelphia are among those that are experiencing such a shortage of teachers that they are looking for qualified candidates in other countries, like Canada and India.[31]

Awareness at the Top

Beyond being "forced" into diversity by demographics, geography, or industry, companies move along the diversity continuum when diversity is embraced at the top of the organization. According to Suzanne F. Kaplan, a diversity consultant to corporations, "Many CEOs understand the business case for diversity—their company's workforce has to look and think like the world at large if they are to be successful in this era of globalization." However, a diversity initiative can also result "when there's a change of heart at the top."

For example, as she explains, "A white CEO learns firsthand from a person of color how different their corporate and life experiences have been, and is touched at a core level and reaches out to widen opportunities in the organization. The executive's lens has been broadened beyond protected, privileged experiences that go along with being white in our society."

Or, "A male CEO who talks a good game in support of women, but has no women on the board or in the top management group, has a change of heart as his own daughter climbs the corporate ladder and hits the glass ceiling. He knows she can add value to her organization. Finally he gets it and suddenly a change of heart occurs," states Kaplan.[32]

With a committed leader at the top, you then choose employees based on a different screening process. Real diversity not only accepts variety, it seeks it out. Rewarding people for making sure there is a diversity of think-ing in the organization is diversity at its best. Real diversity is mental diver-sity.

Movement along this continuum will be critical for employers of the future. I believe that the ultimate goal here goes beyond even the celebration of difference—to a place where differences are irrelevant. Moving forward must include working through tolerance to celebration in the face of diver-sity, even though this continues to highlight differences. Individuals who work for and run companies will need this kind of priority and coaxing toward celebration before they can move to the point where diversity is a non-issue. The mindset of Lindsay and Nneka is a special one; it is ahead of its time. It is the ultimate goal of diversity—to work in a place where we just don't notice the differences anymore.

SELF-SEGREGATION: THE COUNTERTREND TO DIVERSITY

Of course, when the pendulum swings one way, it also swings the other way. There is a countertrend of self-segregation that is creeping across the nation. For example, graduation in May 2003 at the University of Pennsyl-vania included the "2003 Black Senior Celebration" where graduating black seniors gathered to celebrate their uniqueness and special heritage. Before the general graduation ceremony, there were also separate groups celebrat-ing Asian and Latino seniors. Several other colleges and universities are scheduling racially separated graduations along with the general ceremony for everyone. The belief is that these racial and ethnic ceremonies provide a platform to celebrate each group's shared culture and heritage, as well as their ability as a minority to overcome the unique challenges they face at "predominately white universities."[33]

There are others who believe these kinds of celebrations are self-segre-gating. John McWhorter, a professor at the University of California-Berkeley, believes that "campuses are precisely where many black students learn a new separatist conception of being black that they did not have before." I spoke to my daughter about this. She agrees that there has been somewhat of a reversal of diversity on college campuses. Young people are looking for new friends and associations when they go to college. They are on their own for the first time. It is easiest to look for external commonalities, like color or seeing someone at church, when seeking out new companions. It is very natural and not a problem on its own. The problems arise, however, when this self-segregation leads to fear and prejudice.

Further, I believe this countertrend is a movement by various groups to celebrate their uniqueness. African-American, Latino, and gay groups want to stand out as different, separate, and unique in an attempt to restore self-respect for groups that have experienced discrimination.

In another example of the self-segregation countertrend, cities often have ethnic pockets that are proud and passionate about distinguishing themselves from their neighbors. In and around Los Angeles, for example, there are several such areas. African-Americans have lived in South Central for decades. Arcadia is primarily a neighborhood of Indians. Asians live in Little Tokyo, Little Saigon, and Koreatown. West Hollywood is one of the largest gay communities in the nation.[34]

The challenge we face from the countertrend of self-segregation is to remember to celebrate our heritages without allowing the celebration to jeopardize our movement toward a blended society.

LANGUAGE: A HOT TOPIC FOR AMERICA

Signs written in multiple languages seem to create growing fears that English as the primary language of the United States is threatened, but I don't buy it.

There are statistics, mirroring those of immigration, that describe the erosion of English in America. For example, Barbara Wallraff, in her article "WHAT Global Language?" cited that as the proportion of immigrants has grown in the U.S. population, so has the number of people who don't speak English. Spanish-speaking U.S. residents grew by 50 percent in the 1980s, and Chinese-speaking U.S. residents grew by 98 percent.[35] According to The English Company UK, a specialist producer of books and eLearning materials in applied linguistics and English language teaching, by 2050 the world will have:

- ❏ 1,384 million native speakers of Chinese
- ❏ 556 million native speakers of Hindu and Urdu
- ❏ 508 million native speakers of English

❑ 486 million native speakers of Spanish

❑ 482 million native speakers of Arabic

Further, on average, English speakers have lower birthrates than Hindu, Urdu, Arabic, and Spanish speakers. To remain dominant, English must be the language of choice as a foreign or second language.[36]

I do not think that will be a problem. The Internet has kept English dominant throughout the world. Although English is the native tongue to only about 5 percent of the world's population, 75 percent of all Web sites are in English. "No language has ever had this kind of reach and never has there been so much communication between the different corners of the globe," says Justin Fox in a *Fortune* Magazine article "The Triumph of English."[37] English has also long been the world's language for business and science.

Closer to home, English will continue to dominate. As diversity takes hold and the American workforce represents an ever-broadening mixture of people, we will need a common language: English.

CONCLUSION

I believe that the more diverse corporations will be the more successful ones in the future. Ultimately, diversity programs aim to change a corporation's culture, a challenge requiring a comprehensive solution. For example, companies with a large, dispersed workforce will need a multilayered, multifaceted approach to implement a diversity strategy. Companies will need to realize that diversity is strength, not weakness.

The United States in the future will be diverse because that is the kind of country we have created. It sounds simple, but just by eradicating the need for quotas and by people acting responsibly, we will continue to be a greater force.

At the root of a successful organization will be a corporate culture that does not simply have diversity as a policy but that embraces and embodies a diverse workforce as a way to have a productive structure.

Diversity does not yet exist everywhere in the United States, but in regions where there is diversity, new consumer, work, and family life patterns are emerging and leading to many new opportunities. As the competitive landscape intensifies, companies that pay attention to diversity and structure their organizations around it will find that they have far greater access to the best talent pool. This includes men and women, members of different religions, people of many races, disabled persons, and individuals of varying sexual orientation. Truly diverse companies will see opportunities for meaningful contribution from older and younger workers alike, from the disabled, and from those of varying life needs. As organizations move to embrace diversity, they will find that they are ahead of the curve on every measurable front—from recruiting and retaining the best employees to higher profit margins and productivity levels, from better reflecting their marketplace to finally insuring a more satisfying workplace.

NOTES

1. Rodger Doyle, "Assembling the Future," *Scientific American*, February 2002, p. 30.

2. "Whites: A Growing Ethnic Market?" *Forecast,* November 19, 2001.

3. Doyle, op. cit.

4. United States Census Bureau. "Dynamic Diversity: Projected Changes in U.S. Race and Ethnic Composition 1995 to 2050."

5. "Asian Americans and Politics: Perspectives, Experiences, Prospects." *Wilson Quarterly*, Autumn 2001.

6. Andrew Lawler, "Silent No Longer: 'Model Minority' Mobilizes," *Science*, November 10, 2000, p. 1072.

7. Eric Schmitt, "New Census Shows Hispanics Are Even with Blacks in U.S," *The New York Times*, March 8, 2001.

8. *www.aging.unc.edu/infocenter/resources/2000/markidesk/sld004.htm.*

9. *Encyclopedia of American Religions, 7th Edition* (Detroit: Gale Group, 2001).

10. Gustav Niebuhr, "Study Finds Number of Mosques Up 25 percent in 6 Years," *The New York Times*, April 27, 2001.

11. Keith Orndorff, "Assessing American Diversity," *The Futurist*, January/February 2003.

12. Doyle, op. cit.

13. Schmitt, op. cit.

14. "The Birth of an Arab-American Lobby," *The Economist*, October 14, 2000, p. 41.

15. Shannon Henry, "The Widening Pay Gap," *The Washington Post National Weekly*, January 28, 2002, p. 34.

16. "Be a Man," *The Economist,* June 28, 2003.

17. Molly Shepard, interview, September 2003.

18. Lizette Alvarez, "Norway Is Set to Compel Boardrooms to Let More Women In, *The New York Times*, July 14, 2003, p. A3.

19. Molly Shepard, interview, September 2003.

20. Jodie Allen, "Are Men Obsolete?" *U.S. News & World Report*, June 23, 2003.

21. Michelle Conlon, "The New Gender Gap," *Business Week*, Mary 26, 2003, p. 74.

22. Natalie Allen, interview, August 2003.

23. Bill Breen, "Where Are You on the Talent Map?" *Fast Company*, January 2001, p. 102.

24. Timothy Wirth, "Environment & Health: A Connection to the Internet Debate," *Geneva Association Information Newsletter*, November 2000, p. 3.

25. G. Pascal Zachary, "The Global Me: New Cosmopolitans and the Competitive Edge. Picking Globalism's Winners and Losers" (New York: *Public Affairs*, 2000).

26. Weiner, Edrich, Brown Inc., "Critical Combos," June 2003.

27. Zachary, *The Global Me.*

28. Natalie Allen, interview, August 2003.

29. G. Pascal Zachary, "Shortage of Nurses Hits Hardest Where They Are Needed the Most." *The Wall Street Journal,* January 24, 2001, p. A1.

30. Douglas A. Patterson, "The Middle Kingdom," *Vital Speeches of the Day*, January 1, 2001, p. 174.

31. Mary Lord, "Good Teachers: The Newest Imports," *U.S. News & World Report,* April 9, 2001. p. 54.

32. Suzanne Kaplan, interview, September 2003.

33. Michael Fletcher, "Diversity or Division?" *The Washington Post National Weekly*, May 26, 2003, p. 31.

34. Christopher Parkes, "Civic Schizophrenia Leads to Outbreak of 'Lifestyle'," *The Financial Times,* February 27, 2001. p. 7.

35. Barbara Wallraff, "WHAT Global Language?" *The Atlantic Monthly*, November 2000, p.52.

36. Jodi Wilgoren, "Schools Are Now Marketers Where Choice Is Taking Hold," *The New York Times*, April 20, 2001, p. A1.

37. Fox, Justin, "The Triumph of English," *Fortune*, September 18, 2000.

CHAPTER 5

TREND 5: TRUST, RESPECT, AND ETHICS

SEEKING "HIGHER PURPOSE" IN THE WORKPLACE

Throughout my research, the concept of a "higher purpose" continually popped up as a growing movement in business and a rising priority for employees. This caught me somewhat by surprise. While aging and diversity and multigenerational workplaces are common themes of futurists, this sense of higher purpose emerged as something new and unexpected. In a sense, although we weren't looking for it, it came to us on its own.

Higher purpose in the workplace means creating an environment of trust, respect, and ethics where each individual can do his or her best work. According to Edie Weiner, president of Weiner Edrich Brown, a leading futurist consulting group in the United States, "There is the belief that trust, a glue that holds a macro- or micro-society together, is a critical form of social capital, and the more there is of it, the more efficiently people work together."[1]

Employees are seeking a workplace based on trust and on the respect and responsibility that grows from that trust. This type of workplace is made up of informed employees and emphasizes constant, open communication. It encourages the highest and best in each individual employee. Higher purpose in the workplace embodies employee values and a high standard of ethics. Most importantly, the enlightened company lives these values and ethics every day—day in and day out. This is not just a mission statement posted on the wall or an annual donation to a favorite charity. The ethical, principled company is an organization that embraces the respect and trust of each individual.

The workforce of the future will demand something "that is both greater than us and yet within us," describes Sister Mary Trainer, RSM, PhD, who is working with executives and managers of companies to tie work and spirit together in meaningful, ecumenical ways. Trainer says that while many executives and old-school companies find descriptions such as "higher purpose" or "spirituality" hard terms to swallow, they are quite comfortable getting to the same idea through less threatening terms:

❏ Acting with integrity, authenticity

❏ Treating people with dignity and respect

❏ Encouraging a work/life balance

❏ Connecting one's work to a larger sense of meaning and purpose

❏ Creating a culture which embodies core values/ethical principles

❏ Establishing decision-making processes that include reflection on the complex values at stake, and consideration of justice for those affected

❏ Doing business in a socially responsible manner[2]

When organizational leaders act in these ways, they honor the human spirit, and create conditions where people can do their best work, and contribute creatively to the human enterprise. The opportunity for human resources in the organizations of the future is to help companies develop these priorities, which are the essence of higher purpose in the workplace.

I had a recent experience where my outline for an upcoming keynote speech included a segment on "Spirituality in the Workplace." The sponsors balked—this national, highly prestigious organization wanted the topic of spirituality excluded from my presentation. Eventually they acquiesced, and that segment ended up being one of the most effective and meaningful topics for the audience, based on their feedback.

So, whatever we choose to call it—higher purpose or spirituality or trust, respect, and ethics—this is one of our five main trends affecting the workforce of the future. Some would dismiss this idea as a workplace fad that will soon enough go the way of T-groups and Management by Objectives (MBOs). But consider the words of Paul Gibbons in the book *Work and Spirit*:

> Spirituality at Work is a powerful force for good and we who are its custodians must ask ourselves what we are doing to ensure that it is taken seriously and to prevent it from becoming a fad. For if it does become a fad, individuals will have lost the chance to try to apply some well-tested principles and practices in their work lives and to, perhaps, make those work lives more meaningful and joyful.[3]

It is important to note that higher purpose and organized religion are distinctly different. A natural crossover exists between higher purpose in the workplace and diversity that involves reasonable accommodations for the religious requirements of employees, but this does not mean that work is a place of worship. Furthermore, it is most certainly not a place for religious recruitment or mission.

WORKER PRIORITIES ARE CHANGING

Work is a place where people come to do a job and get paid for it. This will probably always remain true; however, the growing importance workers place on personal growth and balance does mean that they want their employment to mean a little bit more. While past research and employee surveys ranked "pay" as a priority goal of their work, current investigations show pay having less importance. As recently as 1980, "pay" was ranked as employees' number one priority, but that began to change in the last decade or so. A 1996 research study from the University of Southern California Marshall School of Business found that "making money" ranked fourth in employee priority.[4] The top three priorities now speak clearly of a shift toward fulfillment, which links to spirituality. The employee priorities at work are, in order:

1. The ability to realize my full potential
2. Working for a good and ethical organization
3. Performing interesting work
4. Making money

Priorities five through seven reinforce the growing movement toward higher purpose:

5. Have good colleagues

6. Provide services to future generations

7. Provide services to immediate communities

TRUST, RESPECT, AND ETHICS START AT THE TOP

Critical to the success of an enlightened workplace are leaders who make upholding these values a priority. These leaders must champion trust, respect, and ethics throughout all levels of the organization. One of the more visible examples of what happens when there is a lack of ethical leadership is Enron. This giant company wrote impressive ethics policies and gave major donations to worthwhile organizations; however, its top executives did not live the core values. Higher purpose comes from within and not from a policy manual.

I serve on the board of the World Affairs Council of Philadelphia, a private, nonprofit, nonpartisan organization dedicated to creating an informed citizenry on matters of national and international significance. It is a wonderful organization with a strong leader, Buntzie Churchill. At lunch recently she shared a story that shows how the culture of respect and ethics must start at the top. One of Churchill's primary responsibilities is raising money, which is especially difficult in these tough economic times. An employee came to her, having found that an individual contributor had paid his membership twice. How should they handle it? As much as the Council needed the money, Churchill did not hesitate. "We sent the money back and told the contributor that he had paid twice," she recounts. Even though they could have used the money, it was returned. This small action carries a powerful message: At all levels of an organization, the culture of ethics must be clear. With a firm commitment at the top to ethics, trust, and respect, an organization can begin to reframe its policies to give much and expect much. Not only was the patron grateful and a little surprised, but the staff too was proud of its organization.

Higher Purpose Close to Home
One of the best examples I have seen of an enlightened leader in a business setting is Alex Johns, chairman and founder of my own organization, CGI Consulting Group, Inc. (CGI) in Malvern, Penn-

sylvania. Here at CGI, he has fostered an environment where people strive to do their best work every day because trust and respect are ingrained in the fiber of the company, as is a sense of fun. Alex maintains this culture without even realizing that it is part of his essence. He is, by nature, a thinker and a teacher. He loves to discuss creative concepts that "push the envelope" with our employees. Alex loves to laugh and share stories—both stories about work with our clients and stories about employees' experiences outside of the office. Through his hearty laugh and his natural teaching and story-telling abilities, Alex continually encourages our employees to learn. As a result, the workplace at CGI abounds with energy and passion. When our employees are asked to describe the company, common words they use are integrity, ethics, true cooperation, and humor. That is, indeed, the essence of higher purpose in the workplace.

June Barry, senior vice president of human resources at Citizens Bank Middle Atlantic Region, describes another excellent example of cultural trust starting at the top. Citizens Bank has a tradition of honoring each 25-year employee with an engraved brick laid at the corporate headquarters in Boston. When Citizens Bank recently bought Mellon Bank, they wanted to have bricks made for those Mellon employees joining the Citizens organization who qualified. No big surprise, some of the employment records hadn't translated perfectly and when a few employees came forward requesting bricks, there was no way to prove they had 25 years of service. At a subsequent meeting, senior officers discussed the issue. How could the records be recaptured? How could the employees' tenure be proved? Just then, the president of Citizens Bank in Philadelphia, Steve Steinour, stopped the conversation and said, "It's easy. If employees say they have been here for 25 years, believe them. Order the bricks." Trust and respect in one simple act.

In talking with so many companies during the course of our research, we find that trust and respect only exist when company leaders embrace it at their very core. More than any other aspects of business we have studied, ethics and respect cannot be delegated or fudged. Lip service will not work. There must be a real commitment and it must start at the top.

Ethics Go Beyond the Letter of the Law

Ethics, trust, and respect go beyond following the law. I find the following example very disturbing. *The Wall Street Journal*, in June of 2003, reported on a practice that I consider, while legal, to be ethically questionable. The article described the fate of Robert Wood, a seven-year employee at a Circuit City store in Florida. Wood was the second-highest-paid salesman at the store, responsible for more than $1 million in computers and electronics sales in one year. Wood and nearly 4,000 other highly paid commissioned sales people were laid off by Circuit City because they made too much money and the company was "desperate to economize."[5]

Circuit City followed up the lay-off by hiring more than 2,000 hourly workers at a much lower pay rate. According to *The Wall Street Journal* report, an increasing number of companies are replacing expensive labor with lower paid workers in order to cut costs. This technique is used by businesses that have jobs that can be easily automated or sent overseas. As I mentioned, it is not illegal to replace expensive workers with lower-paid people, so companies do not have to worry about employment lawsuits. It may not be illegal, but it sure strikes me as lacking trust, respect, and ethics. At the very least, companies need to review such policies. I definitely recommend finding different solutions for increasing the bottom line. There must be better ways to improve profits that do not involve laying off the best performers.

A WORKFORCE OF "BALANCE SEEKERS"

Many Americans are now "balance seekers," looking to create a sense of well-being rather than just building up a hefty bank account. At the same time, however, people are working the equivalent of a month more each year than they did a decade ago. Employees are being asked to give more with less—fewer resources, smaller staffs—and are getting less personal gratification in return. This leads workers to say, "There must be more than this," and to seek balance and deeper meaning in work and life.

Robert Schoonmaker, president of Schoonmaker Associates, Inc., and my husband, has worked for more than thirty years with hundreds of corporate senior executives on life planning. He finds often that the more hours they work, the less rewarding their work becomes. Even the most highly recognized, compensated, and respected executives are searching for something more. Not infrequently, they feel that they have lost their children, having missed their childhoods, and that they have lost their wives or husbands, either literally to divorce, or figuratively as they have become roommates instead of loving partners. Through interviews and exercises, Schoonmaker helps them "find their tugboat"–an expression he coined after finding his own life's passion in refurbishing and piloting his own tugboat at age 70. Time and time again, top executives who have given their all for their companies and seem to "have it all" in return, feel that they have literally gained the whole world and lost their souls.

According to the Gallup Organization National Opinion Research Center, in 1999 a full 78 percent of Americans felt the need to experience spiritual growth in their life–up dramatically from the mere 20 percent expressing the same sentiment in 1994.[6]

Martin Rutte, international speaker and president of Livelihood, a management consulting firm, in his essay "Spirituality in the Workplace" cites three factors that contribute to this growing trend toward higher purpose. First, the aging Baby Boomers, now in their 50s, are reflecting on their lives and their lives' meaning, and are looking to leave their own legacy. They are recognizing that no one ever gets to their deathbed, thinks back, and says "I'm so glad I worked through the weekend on my annual budget each year." Since the Boomers are such a large group, their priorities sway the American population as a whole. As they grow reflective and begin exploring various aspects of higher purpose for themselves, they are providing momentum for an entire trend.

The second factor, according to Rutte, centers on the bio-environment. People have recklessly used and abused our planet for decades–particularly in the 1980s and 1990s. As the pendulum swings the other way, workers are waking up to the fact that good planets are hard to come by, and we all have a stake in taking care of the one we have. Personal efforts to stop littering make some difference, but a greater difference can be made if employees demand that employers be environmentally responsible. This ties to higher purpose in the workplace since workers are placing greater importance on something outside of themselves, something bigger, and they are demanding that their employers do the same.

Finally, Rutte writes of the "maturing" scientific outlook. For centuries, we sought and found answers using science. This has become our paradigm and our method for discovery. Going forward, however, society is finding that some answers lie outside of science. There are no clear and verifiable answers to certain questions—that is when faith and trust (i.e. higher purpose) come into the picture. In a business setting, we see this as culturally ingrained trust, respect, individual honor, and ethics.[7]

Ethics: Of Growing Importance to the Up and Comers

The New York Times described a 2003 survey of MBA students and found that ethical workplace conduct is increasingly important. It was particularly interesting how this study compared to a similar one conducted in 2001. The 2003 study reported nearly 75 percent of students saying that meeting customer needs should be the top priority of a company. Maximizing shareholder value, named by about 70 percent of those polled, came in second. In the 2001 survey, the two were flip-flopped: About 75 percent of MBA students said that increasing shareholder value was a company's top priority, about 70 percent chose meeting customers needs.

Further, students in the 2003 survey went on to describe concerns about some of the curriculum that teaches questionable values. Only about one in five respondents thought their schools were doing "a lot" to help them handle future workplace conflicts involving mismanagement or fraud. One in five said that they were receiving no ethics training at all, and half felt that the messages and priorities taught in MBA programs might have contributed to recent corporate scandals. Harkening back to the discussion on gender in the diversity chapter, where we discussed the importance of what women bring to the table as executive managers: Of the female MBA students surveyed, 82 percent felt it was "very important" for a company to be run "according to its values and a strong code of ethics." Only 72 percent of male students expressed the same priority.[8]

TRUST AND RESPECT AS "SECULAR ENLIGHTENMENT"

As the workforce seeks trust and respect, it also seeks something deeper and more inclusive, which will allow workers to think freely and produce their best work. We call this "secular enlightenment," which acknowledges a deeper need within each of us that comes from our own unique spirit. It includes nonreligious individuals and atheists, as well as deeply religious individuals. Let's take a look at some companies where secular enlightenment is already a reality:

❏ One of the best-known examples is *Xerox Corporation*. Xerox sends employees from all levels of the organization on annual retreats to rural areas, encouraging them to connect with their inner selves and each other, and look for inspiration. The success of this program for Xerox has gone beyond better-centered employees to boost the bottom line. On one such retreat, employees were inspired to create a nonpolluting machine. Upon returning to work, these employees pursued their vision and created one of Xerox's best selling products—a 97 percent recyclable combination digital fax, printer, and copier.

❏ *Donatos Pizza* of Columbus, Ohio, now part of the McDonald's family of companies, created a NEST for its employees—that is, a Nature Enhanced Sound Transmission Sanctuary of Introspection. This special space creates a haven where employees are encouraged to take the time to relax and rejuvenate. Employees are encouraged to use the NEST to recharge tired batteries during their breaks, the time before and after work, and their lunch hours. This is a tremendous testament to the value the company places on the individual and the importance of work/life balance.

❏ At *Rohm & Haas*, a leading manufacturer of specialty chemicals in Philadelphia, a manager offered each of her employees one day off, not part of their vacation allowance, specifically to refresh their spirit. In exchange, she asked for accountability for this day, asking each employee to come back and share their choice, their experience, and the effect it had on them. One of the employees attended a "Work and Spirit Morning" at Cranaleith, a retreat center outside of Philadelphia, whose mission is to create a "contemplative space for all those seeking wholeness and transformation for themselves and society." These morning sessions are designed to provide a creative solution for the person who wants to explore the question "How do I experience the connection between my work and my spirit?" At the end of the day, this employee admitted that she had been skeptical and had gone to the session because she knew it was something her boss recommended. Upon completing the day, however, she came to be grateful for the experience, for herself and for her sense of higher purpose. She was eager to share her experience with her coworkers and to re-approach work from a more centered place within herself.

Performing Social Good

There is an increasing number of "social entrepreneurs," meaning businesses that are starting with socially conscious agendas. Not only are they seeking to do good, they are turning their work into profit. One organization that supports these companies, and in fact is credited with creating the term "social entrepreneurs," is Ashoka. Bill Drayton, an attorney-activist, created Ashoka more than twenty years ago with the mission of funding those who wanted to create business to perform social good. Rather than forming a foundation to simply dole out money, Ashoka sought people with good ideas and the determination to succeed. Then, Ashoka gave them not only monetary grants, but a support network of "Ashoka Fellows." Ashoka now includes more than 1,300 fellows in over forty countries. These fellows include Anil Chitrakar, whose initial Ashoka grants allowed him to set up environmental awareness camps in Nepal.[9]

Dealing with Tragedies

Beyond examples of day-to-day activities bringing higher purpose to work, companies are also bringing trust and respect into the workplace in response to tragedies, such as employee rampages, shootings, industrial accidents, and horrific community events such as the 1999 massacre at Columbine High School. By employing grief specialists and cultivating an openness in the face of tragedy, employers are not just allowing, but encouraging employees to acknowledge hardships that they share as a group. Companies are facilitating community and healing in the face of adversity.

Social Bonding in the Face of Horror

When the terrorists struck on September 11, 2001, most of us were at work. At CGI, we gathered in our conference room to watch the television along with the rest of the world. We waited there together—holding hands—to find out whether one employee's son had made it out of the second tower. We explained that we did not want to offend or force anyone, but just wanted to offer emotional support for our staff. We are fortunate to have one board member who is a minister, so we invited him to say a few words. As we watched the horror mount, we felt the need to do more. He spoke soothingly, sharing hopeful thoughts and guiding us to stay strong—all in a nondenominational, nonreligious way. In the days that followed, several of the employees who were there that day came to us to express the meaningfulness of that spontaneous and spiritual moment.

To put it succinctly, in the words of Laura Nash, business ethicist at Harvard Divinity School and author of *Believers in Business*, "Spirituality in the workplace is exploding." The employees of tomorrow will make sure that a sense of higher purpose envelopes their workplace. I believe the employers of tomorrow had best be aware of it.

HIGHER PURPOSE IN THE WORKPLACE EXPRESSED THROUGH RELIGION

While higher purpose in the workplace does not necessarily involve religion, there are examples of a religious component in the larger spirituality movement. Religion is, for some people and at some companies, an expression of higher purpose. For example, consider the increasing popularity of workplace chaplains:

❑ In the United States, there are about 4,000 chaplains registered in business organizations.

❑ Through a company called Marketplace Ministries headquartered in Dallas, Texas, 250 companies in thirty-five states are employing chaplains as an alternative to more traditional employee assistance programs (EAPs). At least one organization refers to this as their "Employee Care Program."

  ❑ Marketplace Ministries chaplains are trained in the manner of military chaplaincy programs, and are ecumenical in their approach, referring employees who seek specific religious guidance to programs outside the business organization. Their mission is to give guidance, not to create converts.

  ❑ At least 55 percent, and up to 85 percent, of employees talk to the chaplain within the first year of the chaplain coming on board. These same companies found that only 2 to 8 percent of employees used the traditional Employee Assistance Program.

  ❑ No legal complaints have been filed against Marketplace Ministries chaplains.

  ❑ In addition to guidance within the workplace, the chaplains have been asked to perform weddings and funerals for employees outside of work.

❑ According to the Fellowship for Companies for Christ International, more than 10,000 bible and prayer groups meet regularly in companies around the country.

It's not just obscure or small businesses that are employing chaplains. Fast food chains Taco Bell and Pizza Hut, and retail giant Wal-Mart, use chaplains to fill a wide variety of employee needs. The sixth largest franchise of Pizza Hut/Taco Bell in the United States, Austaco, credits its corporate chaplain with a reduction in annual employee turnover from 300 percent to 125 percent—unheard of for fast food companies, which are notorious for high turnover. One Taco Bell employee went so far as to say that she would never leave her job for another one unless the new job included spiritual assistance.

Another fast food chain, Chick-Fil-A, hosts a hymn and prayer service on Monday mornings at its company headquarters in Atlanta for employees who *want* to take part. In one of its most visible commitments to higher purpose and spirituality, Chick-Fil-A restaurants are always closed on Sundays. In more grassroots efforts, the company has sponsored Vacation Bible School programs by providing certificates and coupons for free kids meals.

Traditional Christianity, however ecumenical, is not the only religion inspiring corporate America. New York law firms, such as Kaye, Scholer, Fierman, Hays & Haroller, host Talmud studies. Timberland Shoe Company CEO, Jeffrey B. Swartz, finds managerial inspiration from his orthodox Jewish faith. Nhat Hanh, an internationally known Buddhist monk who teaches non-violence, led a five-day stress management retreat for police officers and other public service employees in Madison, Wisconsin. Deloitte and Touche employees hold prayer groups and the chairman of Aetna International has extolled the benefits of meditation and talked to employees about using spirituality in their careers.[10]

Caveat: Religion in the Workplace

American companies are finding that a growing number of religions are represented in their employee base. In a 2001 survey by the Society for Human Resource Management and the Tanenbaum Center for Interreligious Understanding, 36 percent of respondents (HR professionals) said they see more religions represented in their companies than they did five years ago.[11] With this broadening array of religious representation in the workforce, the more religious expressions of corporate higher purpose will most likely find themselves under pressure to become more secular.

In addition, anything that even *feels* like endorsing or incorporating religion at work gets corporate lawyers up in arms, perhaps with good reason. The number of religious-based discrimination charges jumped 29 percent from 1992 to 1999, according to the Equal Employment Opportunity Commission.

ANOTHER PIECE OF THE ETHICS PIE: SOCIAL RESPONSIBILITY

So what of social responsibility? Companies have seen the importance of good corporate citizenry for years and years. However, they often demonstrate it in highly measurable and publicity-ready ways. They underwrite charitable events—in exchange for prominent banners and program book advertisements. They send disadvantaged youths to camp—along with a corporate photographer to capture the image for posterity and promotion. They offer an "all natural" product line—available only at specialty stores or for a marked-up price.

In very short order, this brand of social responsibility will not be enough. The workforce will demand that social responsibility be inexorably linked to values, company culture, and ethics—a corporate higher purpose. This will be evidenced by the best and brightest of the talent pool seeking out socially responsible companies. As the new workforce becomes more in demand, a company that can share its vision and mission of social responsibility will have an edge with candidates. Examples demonstrating how a company is socially responsible will be a strong recruiting tool. A brochure that highlights the company's social responsibility with testimonials will help attract the best applicants.

HIGHER PURPOSE EXPRESSED THROUGH RITUALS

Within the context of higher purpose in the workplace, there is the phenomenon of rituals. Companies create rituals to cement and celebrate their missions and values. The rituals that were created in companies where trust, respect, and ethics exist were very important and went a long way toward solidifying the caring culture of the organization. On the other hand, rituals in companies without a true ethical culture were seen as a hypocritical joke, actually doing more harm than good. Again this emphasizes that leadership involvement is absolutely critical.

Rituals such as company picnics, employee appreciation days, and chairman's awards are highly effective in companies where the culture starts at the heart and at the top. Once a culture is spiritual, trusting, and respectful, the rituals need not be large or expensive. It does not matter whether a company has a chaplain roaming its halls and making employees feel better or a manager who touches people on the shoulder and remembers to ask about a sick child or an elderly parent. In a spiritual organization, employees may simply and spontaneously gather in the conference room for lunch every Tuesday or buy a group card for birthdays.

Our rituals within CGI, for example, include the large, the small, and the spontaneous. "Feed Back Day" is an annual series of individual meetings where every employee in the company gets an audience with the CEO to discuss the good, the bad, and the ugly. At Family Appreciation Night, we thank employees' families for their role in the success of our employees and our company. Several sunny afternoons after two months of rain prompted "sun time," where each employee was able to take an afternoon off to enjoy the sunshine. The cheers were spontaneous—the cost was nothing.

Another ritual we have created at CGI is the "WAPTA" session, which meets on alternate Tuesdays. Attendance is not mandatory, but nearly everyone chooses to attend. "WAPTA" means "Why Did Alex Pick This Article?" (Alex is Alex Johns, our chairman, described earlier in this chapter.) For each session, Alex chooses a series of recent articles of industry importance or of general interest, from publications such as *The New York Times*, *The Wall Street Journal*, and *The Economist*. Each article is assigned, in turn, to one "WAPTA" attendee who must study it and present it to the rest of the group. From time to time, the question becomes "Why DID Alex Pick this Article?" Everyone has a good time while staying well informed. As a result, employees feel good and strive to do their best.

THE BENEFITS OF WORKPLACE TRUST, RESPECT, AND ETHICS

Companies that are paying attention to trust, respect, and ethics are getting ahead of the curve and are reaping the rewards. In fact, Professor Ian I. Mitroff of the University of Southern California Marshall School of Business goes so far as to say, "Spirituality could be the ultimate competitive advantage."[12] In Mitroff's book, *A Spiritual Audit of Corporate America,* 60 percent of those polled say they believe that there are beneficial effects of spirituality at work, as long as it doesn't include pushing or condoning any specific traditional religion. Employees who feel that their companies are committed to a higher purpose were found to be less fearful, more open to committing themselves to their job, and less likely to compromise on values.

Similarly, "studies have shown that companies that hire and support a workforce with a diversity of ethnic, cultural, and religious backgrounds, as well as those that help employees balance their work and personal lives, experience a variety of business benefits, including:

❑ Increased job satisfaction and employee morale

❑ Increased employee loyalty and commitment

❑ Enhanced productivity

❑ Increased ability to recruit and retain employees

❑ Reduced employee stress

❑ Reduced turnover

❑ Increased ability to access new markets

❑ Enhanced financial performance[13]

There are many benefits to companies embracing the trend toward higher purpose in the workplace. Employees who are less fearful and more trusting are better able to tap their natural creativity more effectively. Regardless of the business role or context, creativity breeds better solutions, which can lead directly to a better bottom line. A sense of higher purpose encourages expression of innate talents, enhances cooperation, and contributes to a sense of loyalty and belonging. This leads to lower turnover, less training, less supervision, and less waste.

CONCLUSION

The persons with whom I spoke about higher purpose and its effects on organizations all expressed a common theme: Companies that promote trust, individual respect, and ethical behavior become employers of choice. Turnover goes down. Loyalty goes up. Savings in recruiting and training are realized. Workers do better work, so profits increase.

Perhaps because the Boomers are getting older and facing their mortality, perhaps because of the violence that we have seen proliferate, perhaps because the time has come to balance the overworked and overindulgent 80s and 90s, the sense of higher purpose is rising. It is rising in the home and it is rising at work. It grows in the form of nondogmatic, noninstitutional belief systems. It grows in the form of demands for personal balance, trust, and respect. Companies that lead and succeed in the future will have strong cultures of trust, respect, and ethics at the core of their organization. In some ways it will be overt, in other ways more subtle, but the spirit of trust and respect, or lack of it, will be the compass that ultimately guides a company.

NOTES

1. Edie Weiner, interview, June 2003.

2. Sister Mary Trainer, interview, July 2003.

3. Paul Gibbons, *Work and Spirit, Spirituality at Work: Definitions, Measures, Assumptions and Validity Claims* (Tonawanda, N.Y.: University of Toronto Press, 2000), p. 128.

4. David Finegold and Susan Mohrman, "What Do Employees Really Want? The Perception vs. the Reality." University of Southern California, The Marshall School of Business: The Center for Effective Organizations. Report presented at World Economic Forum, Davos, Switzerland, January 2001.

5. Carlos Tejada and Gary McWilliams, "Well-Paid Professionals Draw Unwelcome Attention," *wsjonline.com, careersjournal.com.*

6. George Gallup, Jr., and Tim Jones, *The Next American Spirituality: Finding God in the 21st Century* (Colorado Springs, Colo.: National Opinion Research Center, 1999).

7. Martin Rutte, *Spirituality in the Workplace* (Sante Fe, N.M..: Livelihood, 1998).

8. Lynnley Browning, "Ethics Lacking in Business School Curriculum, Students Say in Survey," *The New York Times*, May 20, 2003, p. C-3.

9. "Environmental Camps, Rice Farms, and Hearing Aids: Ashoka Fellows Around the World, *www.knowledge.wharton.upenn,* May 22, 2003.

10. Michelle Conlin, "Religion in the Workplace," *Business Week*, November 1, 1999, cover story.

11. Society for Human Resource Management, "Religion in the Workplace," 2001 survey, *www.tanenbaum.org.*

12. Ian Mitroff and Elizabeth Denton, *A Spiritual Audit of Corporate America: A Hard Look at Spirituality, Religion, and Values in the Workplace* (New York: Jossey-Bass, 1999).

13. Staff, "Religion in the Workplace," Business for Social Responsibility, *www.bsr.org.*

THE IMPACT OF THE TRENDS ON HUMAN RESOURCES

In Part 1, we took an in-depth look at the five major future workforce trends. Whether large or small, public or private, with or without an official HR department, all companies with two or more people, as well as all individual workers, will be affected by these future trends. Now comes the fun part, when we take all that we have lived and experienced, all that we have researched and heard, and consider how what we learned will affect the various disciplines of human resources. In Part 2, we discuss the impact of the trends and provide practical guidance for companies in the future.

To keep on track, I have created a vision statement for the emerging workforce, the workforce of the future.

OUR FUTURE WORKFORCE VISION

In the year 2015, the workforce will:

❑ Live long, healthy, and productive lives and seek meaningful work at age 20, 40, 60, 80, and maybe even 100.

❑ Include as many as five generations working side by side.

❑ Be not only highly diverse, but also highly blended.

❑ Have strong relationships outside of work that may or may not reflect the traditional nuclear family.

❑ Place high priority on integrity and responsibility, requiring a balance of work/life, a work environment of trust and respect, and flexible means to achieve growth-oriented career goals.

CHAPTER 6

THE IMPACT ON HUMAN RESOURCES POLICY

As we consider the impact of the workforce trends on the future of HR management, it is clear that the rules will need to change. So that is where we will start, with HR policies—those hard and fast rules that tell us when to come to work, when to leave, when we can stay home and for how long, who to hire, and who to fire.

In looking at the impact of the trends on HR policy, I will provide several thoughts, suggestions, and examples. Much as each employee is unique, so is each company. Use the ideas that follow to jumpstart your thinking about what might work for you. Try a few. See how they work. I urge you to get outside your comfort zone.

A good place to start is to review current policies and measure them against the emerging workforce trends. Highlight any existing policies that are particularly archaic. These will be the best places to try something new.

HUMAN RESOURCES POLICIES: FROM RULES TO GUIDELINES

Traditionally, policies gave us the answers. It was all spelled out in black and white. In the future, however, the rules cannot be so hard and fast. Companies will need to fill in the black and white with multiple shades of gray.

I like to think of myself as somewhat of a pioneer in the gray area of HR policy. Way back in the 1970s, I was director of benefits for ARAMARK, a large company of more than 230,000 employees. I managed more than 2,000 health and welfare plans and sixty-nine defined benefit pension plans, and it sometimes felt as if I were managed by almost the same number of bosses. I was on my eighth boss in seven years when I became pregnant. This boss, Scotty Campbell, was an older gentleman, who had been President Carter's director of personnel. I did not know much about him yet, nor he about me, but I figured he was pretty "old school." For five months I hid my pregnancy —wearing my blouses out instead of tucked in. Since he did not know me, he had no reason to guess I was pregnant. Finally, the day came when it was time to tell him. I effused about my commitment to work and my hope that I had proven myself to him in our short time together. He was very kind and supportive.

Five weeks after I delivered my daughter, Scotty called me at home to ask my counsel on a particularly sticky pension subject—using pension assets to help buy company stock for a management buy-out to take the company private. This required more than my telephone counsel; it was a huge project and I had to get back to work. My mother watched the baby and off I went—a 42-mile commute each way. As time went on, I found a nanny so the baby could stay home. Still, I needed time to regroup each week, so I devised the "Hankin Plan." With only my secretary in the know, I worked at home on Wednesdays. I could be with the baby in the morning and afternoon, stay in my sweats, and still put in a full day of work by telephone and dictation. Six months into my experiment, I asked Scotty to lunch.

"So, Scotty, I just want to be sure that you are happy with how things are going with my performance since I have returned to work," I started the conversation easily.

"I'm thrilled! I have to be honest that I am a little surprised—in my generation, the women always stayed home to raise the children."

"Have you noticed that I have not been in the office on Wednesdays?"

"That just can't be true," he replied, dumbfounded.

"It is true! I switch my days anytime you need me, but basically I hold my meetings by telephone on those days. I still have my nanny, so I am not interrupted while I work, but I needed the leeway to not make the commute or get dressed up one day a week. Plus, I have all that extra time with my child."

I went on, hardly stopping for breath. "For the privilege of working from home on Wednesdays, I am willing to take a 20-percent cut in my pay, retroactive to the day of my return from leave. I will announce it to the entire company, particularly my staff. You will get more than five days of work for an 80-percent salary. I will get time with my daughter."

Talk about gray! That was about the shade of Scotty's face at first. "I'll think about it," he managed to say once the shock wore off enough that he could respond. "No, wait. I don't need to think about it. This is the way of the future. Let's see if it works."

I insisted on taking the pay cut as a way to make this a win-win for both of us. I absolutely felt it was worth the sacrifice in order to get what I needed: time with my baby. Scotty Campbell was ahead of his time. This shade of gray worked for me and, subsequently, for many others at ARA-MARK who followed my lead.

So what are some of the general ways companies can add a bit of flexibility—some gray shading, if you will—to HR policies in recognition of the changing needs of the new workforce of the future?

NO SET SCHEDULES

Allow employees to come and go as they need, and establish schedules that work with their lives. Consider these facts:

- ❏ Elderly people are often up before dawn. As such, seniors may prefer to come to work very early in the morning and finish by noon.

- ❏ Young people often do their best work at night. A 2000 study by Duke University showed that the most common time a college student is on the computer is 2 A.M. Yet right after graduation, they are forced into a 9-to-5 routine.

- ❏ Moms and Dads might like the chance to break up their workday in order to shuttle children to lessons, help with homework, or attend a game.

Rather than watching schedules and monitoring lateness, watch productivity and monitor results. Rather than chastising an employee for chronic lateness, check into the situation and adjust your expectations.

Chronic lateness could be unavoidable for a single parent who needs to get children on the bus before they can leave for work. On the other hand, it could be an indirect cry for help from an employee in the grip of substance abuse. In these types of sensitive situations, it is important to get to know the employee before you take action. Still, policies that seek to support rather than punish will help all employees do their best work.

BROADEN THE AVAILABILITY OF PERSONAL TIME

Consider turning personal days into personal-time allotments. Employees may need a few hours one morning for a doctor's appointment for themselves or a loved one. It may be planned ahead or result from an emergency. Personal time may require an hour here or there, a day or two, even weeks.

Provide guidelines for what is a reasonable standard and a means to find solutions to unique situations outside the guidelines. Offer alternatives such as making up the work, making up the time, or working from a different location. Employees in certain situations may rather take a cut in pay and hours than be chastised and disciplined for violating a set policy.

PRESERVE VACATION TIME

Rather than demanding that an employee caregiver use all of their vacation time to accommodate demands of a personal situation, carve out a different solution. An employee who is being pulled in several directions both inside and outside of work is especially in need of downtime to de-stress and rejuvenate—the original purpose of vacation. Don't take that away from them.

At CGI, we call this kind of situation a "Life Moment." We've all had them. One year I shuttled back and forth from Philly to Florida to help my Dad care for my Mom, who had both cancer and Alzheimer's. I still had work, and my youngest child was applying for college at the same time. I needed flexibility, understanding, and empathy for my "life moment." When it was over, I was back with a renewed spirit for the company.

POLICIES OF THE FUTURE MUST BE OPEN

The above headline is simple to write. The delivery is much more complex. Effective companies in the future will need to manage their HR policies with a firm but open hand—"open" enough to allow for flexibility, creativity, and using group as well as individual solutions. Here are a couple of examples of what we mean:

❑ *Planned Company Closings.* Closing the company for certain days each year gives everyone a chance to stop and take a breath. Holidays are great for this. Their original intent of closing in recognition of a certain event or remembrance has largely been replaced by a simple day off or long weekend. Sometimes holidays themselves can even create a degree of stress.

Consider closing periodically out of respect for your employees' hard work and in recognition of their ongoing loyalty and commitment to company success. Quarterly closings for a long weekend tied to no holiday may make sense, or closing the company for a few days or even a week after completion of a certain season or project. For example, an accounting firm could close for a week after tax season. A manufacturer could give employees a four-day weekend after filling its fall orders.

❑ *Employee-Set Holiday Schedules.* Beyond the planned company closings, employee time-off for holidays should be made available. Instead of the company closing for Christmas, forcing Jewish or Islamic employees to use vacation time for their own religious holidays, employees should instead be given a holiday allotment. The employees designate the holidays that they will recognize for the upcoming year. Perhaps an interim solution is a half-and-half holiday policy: a few company-designated holidays and the rest as personal choice holidays.

Open Policy at Work Today
In the June 2003 issue of *Inc.* there was an article profiling a company called TechTarget.[1] Located in Needham, Massachusetts, this interactive media company has more than 200 employees—all of whom are free to come and go as they please. The founder and CEO of the company is Greg Strakosch, a self-proclaimed "hater" of bureaucracy and set policies.

TechTarget has *no* policy setting work hours or sick time. Employees work when they feel they can be most productive, even if that is in the middle of the night. Personal and vacation days also are up to the individual employee. Instead of dictating when and how an employee works, TechTarget is all about results. Armed with quarterly goals and timetables, employees are largely independent about when and how to achieve them. Employees must stay in ongoing communication with their bosses and be accessible by phone and computer to answer questions and give updates.

Naturally, there are limits. For example, an employee cannot call in Monday morning to say he or she will be out for the week. Also, under-performance or abuse of the openness results in termination. As I would expect, the trust and commitment are returned manyfold. The *Inc.* article reports the accolades from employees who are mothers of young children and others who are hard-core athletes in training. Many workers reportedly put in at least fifty hours a week. The company is just four years old and is doing very well—revenue went up approximately 30 percent from 2002 to 2003. We will watch with great interest how these open policies can continue and flourish as TechTarget becomes a larger company.

THE CHANGING FACE OF HUMAN RESOURCES

Human resources in the future will evolve and expand. HR professionals will become the "strategic solutionists." They will need to be both knowledgeable and creative in their approach to balancing unique employee needs and company goals and objectives for productivity and profitability. They will need to devise strategies and solutions for a growing number of new and developing situations.

This will require additional training for both HR professionals and line managers. As much as line managers will need to become more active in human resources, HR managers will need to become more cognizant of the business and industry of the company. HR professionals will offer practical, sometimes almost customized guidance that will replace policy manuals. They will champion both individual employee situations and company goals. Employees, too, will need to become involved in the process— educated as to the openness of the guidelines as well as the expectations from them in return.

Here are some of the new directions human resources will need to take in the future:

❑ *Commit to Openness in Writing.* Most of the vision and mission statements I have seen do not include reference to HR policy, but I'm sure it is coming. In order for openness, flexibility, and creativity vis-à-vis employee needs to be germane to company process, they need to be incorporated into the mission and vision statements by which a company defines itself.

❑ *Involve Employees in Determining Policy Guidelines.* When revamping policies from rules to guidelines, finding the balance will be a challenge. To see what's reasonable and important to employees, just ask them. Employee focus groups are not a new concept, but using employee focus groups to influence HR-policy guidelines is brand new. At CGI, we often utilize employee focus groups when we engage a new client and are in the beginning stages of benefits redesign. I am often amazed at how thoughtful and reasonable employees are when entrusted with company-related strategy development.

Five Questions to Ask Employee Focus Groups on Policy
Keep all questions open-ended in order to generate discussion. Use an outside facilitator if at all possible. Have separate sessions for management and employees. Aim for twenty or fewer attendees per focus group for best discussion. Use flip charts to record notes with no specific attributions. Release results of focus groups.

1. What do you like best about working here?
2. What do you like least about working here?
3. What would enable you to do your job better?
4. When your group/department works at its best, what does that look like? What's happening?
5. What three things would you change about the company that would enable you to be more satisfied?

❑ *Ask Employees for Specific Solutions.* Managers and HR professionals are not the only ones with answers. When a company crisis arises, employees are often the best at creative solutions. When faced with the next dilemma, ask the workers for potential solutions. You may be surprised at how imaginative and useful some of the responses are.

At CGI a few years ago, an ice storm had paralyzed our region. CGI closed, as did all schools and most companies. Within a couple of weeks, a second ice storm hit, and we closed again. Predictions called for several more ice storms in the coming weeks. We called our employees together and expressed how we could not continue to close—we needed to service our clients' employees around the country. Human resources and senior management were at a loss for a solution, so we asked employees for ideas. Their solution: Employees owning SUVs but who were not willing to drive in ice lent them to employees willing to drive them in the nasty weather. The volunteer drivers drove the SUVs home the night before a predicted ice storm and then picked up stranded employees and their children the next day. Since clients weren't coming in due to the storm, the conference room was filled with games, toys, and videos, becoming an ad hoc day care center staffed by teenage children of employees. Food was brought in. We successfully stayed open for the next thirteen ice storms. Parents felt secure. Teens made money. Clients were serviced. It was a "win" for everyone, and the idea came from employees, not management.

❑ *Employee Judiciary Committee.* One of the management fears concerning open policy programs is that they will be ripe for abuse. Guidelines help employees and allow for flexibility that builds trust, respect, and loyalty. Rather than painting management into the corner of deciding how much is too much or when flexibility becomes abuse, an employee judiciary committee can serve as arbitrator. Grievances can be filed by employees or by managers who feel that abuse of the policy guidelines is taking place. Both parties need to agree to be bound by the decision of the committee. Committee members should rotate periodically and reflect a broad range of employees. Members might volunteer, be elected, or be appointed.

❑ *Dress Codes as a Two-Way Street.* Everything was so simple when all the men wore white shirts, suits, and ties, and the women wore skirts. Most employees have welcomed the recent trend toward casual dress, across the board. When we have asked our employees to name the best things about working at CGI, casual dress always makes the list. They feel more comfortable; they save money; they feel more productive. Loosening dress codes welcomes a divergence of style and culture. It allows for individual expression.

The flip side, however, is that some people "go too far" and offend other employees with their dress. This actually can get pretty dicey. If a Muslim employee can wear a turban, can a white supremacist wear a swastika? How much skin is too much? How many tattoos are too many? What about face piercings? Why should we get bogged down in such matters?

One solution is to provide reasonable guidelines, with employee input, and have the employee judiciary committee determine cases that "go too far."

Employers may also find that simple company uniforms are a more effective means of balancing and equalizing a diverse range of employees. Parents and students who fought school uniforms as a crushing blow to individual expression are finding instead that they are a welcome and cost-effective relief. Several high tech companies in the Silicon Valley started this with golf shirts with the company logo for everyone.

❑ *Business Referral Policy.* The more employees are involved in the success of the company, the more committed and loyal they will be. Business referral policies that reward employee involvement in finding new business for your company build a close relationship and enhance company loyalty.

Sample Business Referral Policy

This is the "formal" policy for bringing new business to CGI:

One of the best avenues for new clients is business referral. Our employees can be an important resource for such referrals. If you know of a possible business/client lead, share it with the Marketing Department.

Plan A: I Want to Be a Salesperson
For bringing in and working with a prospect until the prospect becomes a client the following will apply: We will pay you a commission equal to a percentage of our collected fees for consulting and administrative services, other than installation or set-up charges, and commissions which we earn with respect to such client, for a three-year period.

Plan B: Finder's Fee
A finder's fee of $1,000 will be paid to any employee who refers a prospect to CGI and the prospect becomes a client. This can come from an old client you have stayed in touch with, or from a brand new source, but not a split of a current client.

Plan C: Boy, Is CGI Lucky!
Zero percent for house leads that come from the good work of the people that work here. This means that if a current client moves to a new company and calls in to the sales department directly, no one gets referral money.

HUMAN RESOURCES POLICY AND THE FIVE TRENDS

We've looked at some general ideas companies can use to open up HR policy and allow employees more flexibility, participation, and input. Now let's take a closer look at specific ways companies can adapt HR policy to the five emerging workforce trends.

IMPACT OF LONGEVITY ON HUMAN RESOURCES POLICY

Older employees bring many special benefits to the workplace, but they also have different needs from younger members of your workforce. As workers are active into their 80s and 90s, company policy will need to accommodate them. Here are some things to consider:

❑ *Nap Policies.* Providing a quiet, darkened area as well as allowing employees the time to take a nap can help boost productivity and employee loyalty. Besides older workers, others that can benefit from this flexibility in their daily schedule are pregnant employees and those recovering from surgery.

❑ *In-House Medical Support Policies.* In-house medical support will supplement health-care benefits and be important to employers who want to support their older employees in ways that allow them to stay at work. Companies may find that hosting an on-site infirmary more than pays for itself through the decrease in time away from work due to illness. Flu shots, nutrition counseling, weight management support, and other resources can be included. Senior employees who are independent but don't have the support system of a spouse or children at home to help them when they are sick will especially benefit. A 24-hour nurse hotline can field questions and offer advice that helps older employees stay healthy and at work. A policy of providing employees who are losing their hearing with high volume phones can increase worker satisfaction and effectiveness.

❑ *Convenience Policies.* Conveniences will help senior employees who are quite self-sufficient and effective at work, but who are limited in their ability to access outside resources. Possible conveniences are:

  ❑ A company store for incidentals and necessities would save all employees time running errands, but would especially help those older workers who are less mobile.

  ❑ A concierge service can provide conveniences such as pickups from cleaners or pharmacies.

  ❑ Providing transportation could help in the same way. Facilitating a system where younger employees pick up older ones would remove a large burden from the shoulders of the aging workers and build relationships across the generations.

  ❑ Shuttle buses or van pickups from senior housing to work and back could also be attractive. These shuttles could also take employees to day-time doctor appointments, with flexible scheduling allowing them to make up the time.

❑ In-house cafeterias are common in large companies. In the future, this convenience can expand to a service of providing hot meals for employees to take home. Older employees who live alone or may be less able to cook for themselves will especially appreciate this policy, as will busy parents who don't have the time to prepare full meals at home.

❑ *Social Activities and Classes.* For older employees, social lives can be heavily tied to their jobs. Policies that provide for company-sponsored social activities will become more prominent. These could include everything from cards to bingo to square dancing. Knowing the importance of balance as we age, companies with a priority on employee wellness can begin company-sponsored yoga and tai chi. Company-sponsored self-defense and safety courses can benefit all employees, not just senior ones.

❑ *Advocates Policy.* Keeping senior workers focused and active will mean keeping them in good standing on several fronts where tales of "elder abuse" run rampant. A buddy system could provide employee advocates to go along to doctor appointments, to meetings with lawyers for reviewing wills or other legal documents, or to car-buying appointments. Financial advice and identity theft prevention tips can also be provided.

IMPACT OF MULTIPLE HOUSEHOLD TYPES ON HUMAN RESOURCES POLICY

The increasing number of household types will require policies that allow employees to define "family" and that support that definition. Companies will find that here, too, flexibility is the key.

❑ *Family Appreciation Day.* Consider hosting a day that celebrates and unites all things that mean family for your employees. This inclusive event should go beyond activities for kids and allow employees to not only invite but also celebrate their family, which could include aging parents and other relatives, housemates, same-sex partners, and maybe even pets.

❑ *Preregister for Bereavement Leave.* Employees register the name and relationship of those whom they consider "immediate family" and "extended family." Guidelines will provide parameters. In the event of the death of a registered family member, the employee is entitled to appropriate bereavement leave without question or concern.

❑ *Expand the FMLA (Family Medical Leave Act).* A company can broaden its definition of who is included/recognized under FMLA. In cases of single parents, companies should consider allowing single parents or caregivers to take double family leave, since if both a mother and father worked for the company, they would each be entitled to separate 12-week leaves.

Family Support Policies

❑ *Tutors.* Companies can use internal resources and employee volunteers as tutors for employees and their children. These tutors could be available to anyone from children being raised by grandparents who are employees, to elders who need help with computer equipment.

❑ *Homework Help.* This kind of network can be similar to tutors, but rather than being formal and ongoing, employees volunteer to be "on call" for certain subjects for which employees or their children may have an immediate question. For example, someone in the accounting department may be available to answer math homework questions for an employee's child who is stumped by the assignment. A coworker pursuing an advanced degree who has a math question could call upon that same employee.

❑ *School Applications Assistance.* Company support can include assistance and advice on completing college applications, or uncovering and pursuing scholarship and financial aid opportunities. Translators can be available to help relatives and employees whose primary language is not English.

❑ *Leases, Rental Agreements, Buying Agreements, Mortgage Assistance/ Advice.* Similarly, companies can support employees who are navigating the potentially overwhelming complexity of legal documents, such as leases, rental agreements, and mortgages. The internal legal department could expand to provide assistance or an outside provider could assist.

❑ *Financial Planning Assistance.* An increasing array of household types will be challenged with a wide variety of budgetary and time management concerns. Companies can provide in-house financial planning assistance, or set up an agreement with an outside provider.

❑ *Help Caring for Sick Relatives.* Companies can consider a broad range of support policies for employees responsible for the care of sick relatives. Allowing employees to bring them in or work from home would be a help. Employers can arrange for in-home nurse care or develop a drop-in sick center arrangement with a nearby medical facility/hospital, where employees can drop off sick relatives during work. Sick leave may be redefined to include sick relatives, not just sick employees.

❑ *Support Groups.* Companies can facilitate the creation of support groups for employees with different needs. These could include single fathers, grandparents raising children, parents going through adoption, gay parents, or employees with a relative suffering from Alzheimer's. These support policies will be different from an Employee Assistance Program (EAP), because they will be internal, ongoing, and unlimited in the number of meetings permitted.

❑ *Scheduling Flexibility.* Probably the most pervasive change that will be required by the numerous types of households is flexibility in scheduling. Scheduling flexibility will include part-time schedules, working from home, job sharing, and other increasingly common accommodations, but will also go further. A part-time worker who is a parent may work four shorter days a week during the school year in order to be home when the children get off the bus. Then, when summer comes, three full-time days a week, while the children are at camp, may be better.

❑ *Working Outside the Office.* Telecommuting, per say, is not new. The broadening array of the types of workers and positions for working outside of the office, as well as the reasons for those types of flexible arrangements, will be new. Working in places other than the office may become the rule, not the exception. Home offices won't be the only option either. Working from the library, a coffee shop, or a senior citizens home will become increasingly common. Writing this book allowed me to see that certain kinds of work can be accomplished literally anywhere. This book has been edited on airplanes, on the kitchen table, at restaurants, and on the beach. This won't work for the job I do in front of clients, but it can work for my behind-the-scenes work. Results are what matter. Results and timelines will be monitored by the on-site managers.

Making the "Switch" to Telecommuting

ARO Call Center handles customer service for financial and insurance companies, like CitiGroup and AIG. Several years ago, ARO started a telecommuting program as part of an initiative to reduce a huge 60-percent employee turnover rate. Recruiting and training costs were much too high and the company's worker base was largely young and inexperienced. A November 2001 article in *Business 2.0* describes how ARO put nearly $1 million into a new switch system that acts as an operator and allows employees to telecommute simply by having two phone lines.[2] For example, when a customer calls the CitiBank toll-free number, the switch recognizes the number and routes the call to an agent trained to handle CitiBank clients. The results for the company have been wonderful. The article reported that 85 of 100 agents work from home, and that the annual turnover rate dropped to 5 percent. Moreover, the employees tend to be older and have significant work experience, and they can handle 20 percent more calls than were handled before the switch system was in place. Even operating costs dropped about 30 percent, partially due to the decrease in office space rental. There are lots of win-win solutions out there, but no one solution for everyone. It takes willingness to try, creative ingenuity, and—I'll say it again—flexibility.

Impact of Multiple Generations on Human Resources Policy

The multiple generations represented in the workforce of the future will present many opportunities for creative thinking on the part of HR professionals and management. There is much to be gained by encouraging cross-generational cooperation and teamwork. Companies must also be aware of the possible friction points when generations mix in the workplace.

Here are some ideas for establishing specific HR policies in light of the multigenerational workforce:

❑ *Generation Gap Grievance Roundtables.* Whether for older workers with younger bosses, or recent grads whose supervisor is a "dinosaur," round table discussions for grievances can enhance communication. These allow members of different generations who work together to sit with others of various ages from throughout the company and share concerns in an open environment that can bridge the gap.

❑ *Generation Buddies.* Similar to mentors, but less "official," a buddy system across generations can help employees of different ages learn to appreciate each other, find what makes different generations tick, and help them know how to better communicate across generations. There is also the chance here to open things up to a little two-way "mentoring." For example, older workers can offer knowledge gained from their experience, while younger computer-literate employees can offer technical guidance. Both generations gain from this kind of interaction. Spread throughout the workforce, it can strengthen your company in many ways, large and small.

❑ *Brown-Bag Lunches with Generational Speakers.* Employees can gather in a conference room once a month to discuss different topics that help educate the various generations about one another. Fellow employees can serve as guest speakers. For example, a younger worker could be invited to explain new jargon, or what's "hot and hip," to older workers. An older worker could be invited to share insights about historical events that predate many younger workers, share company history stories, or perhaps outline traditional etiquette and manners that have fallen by the wayside.

❑ *Flexible Hours for Exercise or Physical Therapy.* Each generation could take advantage of the opportunity to take care of their personal needs.

❑ *Making Many Forms of Policies/Records Available.* While being mindful of privacy, it will be important to make company information, updates, policies, and even personnel records available in many forms, including on an intranet, the Internet, a portable CD, audio, or in large-print format.

❑ *Volume Control Policy.* Some workers may be hard of hearing, some make speak very loudly, others may listen to loud music. Consider developing guidelines for considerate volumes and noise levels.

❑ *Offer Alternatives.* Provide workspaces where employees can go and be respectful of others. For example, employees can sit in a small conference room when making several calls in a row or when they need privacy. Encourage personal music devices with headphones, if appropriate to the work place.

Impact of Diversity on Human Resources Policy

Someone once told me that the best advice you could give to a manager is to ask her to hire someone who is her complete opposite, thus not only increasing diversity but also balancing points of view, experiences, and skill sets. The days of the "cookie-cutter" hiring to fit some corporate image are long gone—and good riddance. Companies will find strength in the diversity of their workforces. Policies developed to accommodate the increasingly diverse workforce will allow employees to appreciate each other, learn about rather than fear differences, and open lines of communications.

Seeking Inclusion
I attended a Multiple Sclerosis (MS) luncheon fundraiser where a twenty-seven-year-old female lawyer shared her story. This woman learned she had MS one month before her wedding. Undaunted, she got married as planned. Then, she set out to learn all she could about this disease that was now playing such a prominent role in her life. She explained that now every day is a mystery—she never knows how or what she will feel when she wakes up. Sometimes she'll have triple vision or hearing loss in one ear. Sometimes she is unable to use one or both legs, or her hands feel like fifty tons of dead weight. Sometimes, she wakes up and feels just fine. She said

she works hard every day that she feels well, since she never knows what the next day will bring.

She then went on to describe a time when she didn't attend the company picnic. Her concerned coworkers asked why she didn't attend. In short, she responded, the heat was the culprit. She could no longer go to a picnic in 90-degree heat and 90 percent humidity.

This story led me to realize that diversity issues are so much broader than we may initially think. The more we are educated about different religions, gender issues, cultures, and handicaps, the more we can be sensitive not to offend, but also able to create inclusion. For example, providing an air-conditioned tent or nearby shelter could have allowed this dedicated worker to attend the company picnic.

Here are some policy ideas forward-thinking companies are already using today to help incorporate diverse workers into the fabric of their organizations:

- ❏ *English as a Second Language.* ESL can be company-sponsored courses that assist foreign-born employees and their families through either in-house or outsourced programs. Literacy tutoring can be supported the same way.

- ❏ *Developing Expanded Job Profiles.* Completing competency profiles of jobs and accessibility profiles of jobs will facilitate recruitment of disabled or handicapped individuals.

- ❏ *Tolerance Awareness Groups.* A group of employees from multiple backgrounds can be formed to set guidelines for acceptance, develop educational/awareness programs, and serve as a place for employees to bring concerns and ideas to make the workplace more accepting.

- ❏ *Harassment Policy Awareness Day.* Hosting a day-long event where everyone in the company is made better aware of what constitutes harassment—whether based on age, sex, handicap, or cultural differences—can make a major contribution toward improving understanding and sensitivity to differences.

- ❏ *Representation in Management.* Insuring that a diversity of thinking and input is happening at all levels of the organization will require proactive initiatives. These can include Proactive Succession Planning that actively seeks diverse employees for long-term training and grooming for company management. Outsourced Succession Planning by an outside firm can be done "blindly" by phone, paper, and/or computer. This allows the obvious racial or handicap appearance not to sway a decision.

- ❏ *Seeking Diverse Input.* Until board rooms and executive teams reflect the diverse base of their employees, companies will need to create policies that invite diversity into thinking, planning, and decision making. Inviting participation from diverse employees on various task forces and project teams helps broaden views in the short-term.

- ❏ *Employee Library and Resource Center.* This can be a very useful way of supporting the diverse workforce. Books, magazines, how-to's, and software tutorials can address a variety of business issues and be available for workers to check out.

IMPACT OF TRUST, RESPECT, AND ETHICS ON HUMAN RESOURCES POLICY

In a nutshell, seek to blend home and work to make life easier to accomplish in a balanced way. Remember, it doesn't have to cost money to show you trust and respect your employees. To a large extent, all the policy ideas we've described establish a culture of trust and respect. Here are some others:

- ❏ *Confidentiality Policy.* This can include annual HR records purging of what is no longer needed and employee review of their own personnel folder.

- ❏ *Employee Access to Private Rooms and Phones.* Especially as workspaces are more open, with more cubicles than walls, employees need to have conference rooms or other areas where they can feel free to make personal phone calls when they are of a sensitive nature.

❑ *Community Support Policies.* While policies must provide open avenues to trust and respect individual privacy, they must support employees' needs for community. When the work world is complicated either by positive events, such as landing a big case or a new client, or by tragic events, such as natural disasters, war, or terrorism, HR structure must support and respect employees through these events even as it enables the organization to move forward. Impromptu meetings, scheduled updates, blast e-mails, and company newsletters are just a start. A culture that allows employees to drop what they are doing and come together in times of need is also important.

Fear of Policy Abuse: Not to Worry

It is quite natural to fear that all this openness to creative solutions will just lead to widespread abuse by employees. No one will come in on time. They will come and go as they please. They will lie and cheat the system. As a result, productivity and profits will plummet. I strongly believe, however, that this will not be the case at all, for the following reasons:

◆ First of all, I have seen open systems of trust and respect work not only in our own company, but also in other organizations such as TechTarget and ARAMARK.

◆ Second, it is vital to keep in mind that open HR policy requires priority emphasis on quality results and timelines. While future policies must allow for individual support, such as work/life balance, scheduling, or environmental accommodations, it must also set goals for results, quality, and deadlines. Instead of measuring when you come in, when you leave, or where you sit, companies will need to measure how much work is done, how well it is done, and how timely it is done.

◆ Finally, in return for policies that are more open and based on trust and respect, employers will enjoy two tremendous benefits from employees in exchange: commitment and tenure. By commitment, I mean an employee's emotional attachment to the company and its success. By tenure, I mean an employee's length of employment and unwillingness to leave the company. Both are critical to company success in the future even more so than today.

- ❏ *CEO Breakfasts.* Executives can host monthly breakfasts with employees chosen at random from different levels and departments of the organization. Normally, a manager would not attend with an employee. At these casual gatherings, the CEO can present a brief company update/overview and answer any questions that employees may have. After that, no more business talk! It will be a time for the CEO and employees to get to know each other as people.

- ❏ *Business Retreats at Homes of Managers.* Inviting small groups of employees to the homes of managers can work well for offsite meetings. This opens up the more personal side of the executives, and positions them as more human and less intimidating.

- ❏ *Meditation Centers.* In addition to the infirmary, employers can offer a spot where employees can go to be away from it all and to gather their thoughts. This could be a private outdoor courtyard, or a darkened room with plants, soft music, and fountains. Benches, mats, and cushions, as well as some form of screens for privacy would be important considerations.

- ❏ *Sabbatical Programs.* At CGI we once tried a sabbatical program. The concept was this: Upon an employee's tenth anniversary, that individual could take three months off at full pay in order to do something that would enrich his or her life. We felt that this was a great reward and an exceptional retention tool, allowing employees to pursue an exciting adventure or life-long dream without having to leave our company. Of course, we designed this program when our company was only a few years old. By year eight, we started getting worried. We were still a relatively small company, and each employee was so valuable that the idea of covering a vacancy for three months seemed nearly impossible. In fact, by year ten some people were able to take their sabbatical and indeed loved it, while others chose not to take it or just added a day or two to vacations until they used up their time. It was a wonderful idea, it was tried, and it may go away, but at least we were experimenting with new policies.

❑ *Open Policy of Sharing Company Information.* I call this the "blab it all out" theory—share what is going right, what is going wrong, client updates, company financial updates, new business/prospect updates, employee updates (mindful of privacy issues). This sets the tone for the company as being one that is trusting and respectful.

❑ *Feedback Day.* Hosting an annual sit-down with employees where there is an open platform to share the good, bad, and ugly, can demonstrate a huge commitment to employee respect and trust. More important than the meeting itself, however, is what happens after it—does management follow up on what's been aired, are changes made, is there any retaliation against workers who spoke out, etc.

❑ *Morale Committee.* At CGI we call them the Live Wires. At The STAR Group they are the Goalkeepers. Whatever the name, the concept is the same—an internal committee of employees that creates employee fun and events. Some ideas include drawings for little prizes, hosting an employee barbeque, passing out green "Shamrock Shakes" for St. Patrick's Day, little appreciation notes for Valentine's Day, or passing out bags of peanuts that say "We know it's been nuts around here. Thanks for your help." Sometimes a gesture that seems almost trivial on the surface can boost morale across the board.

❑ *Appropriate Use of Company Resources for Private Use.* Within reasonable guidelines, employees can use company resources, such as copiers or postage machines, for their private use. Up to a certain point, this can be free to employees.

❑ *Managers Retrained to Focus on Results, Not Hours.* This takes a tremendous shift in mindset, but it is one of the most important ways that a company can walk the talk of trust and respect. The company itself must start by revamping its policies and communicating the changes to employees and managers alike.

❑ *Job Descriptions.* Rather than a list of activities to describe a job, link compensation directly to a list of expected results. Unless absolutely critical to the job, eliminate education/years of experience requirements.

❑ *360° Feedback That Is More Specific and Less Anonymous.* I have found and heard from others that 360° feedback is much more open, respected, and effective when participants are encouraged to be specific and stand behind their comments.

❑ *Car Wash Day.* I throw this idea in just for fun. Research shows that a having a clean car boosts one's mood. Plus, it can be a terrific team-building exercise. Maybe just give employees coupons to the local car wash as an "on the spot" bonus.

TREATING EVERYONE FAIRLY VS. TREATING EVERYONE THE SAME

While I am a strong proponent of treating all employees fairly, I want to point out that this is not the same as treating all employees the same. We inherently know this does not work. We do not treat our own children the same. This is because every child is different and has different needs. This carries into the workplace. In a context of trust and respect, fairness means determining the best course for the individual. Policies need to be developed that allow for individual solutions, but are fair.

This reminds me of a recent encounter I had with my stepson, Rick. Rick is in his mid-40s, his wife is the primary breadwinner, and they have three children, two cars, one mortgage, one dog, and one rabbit. Rick works for a large generator-repair company. Since his wife does not get home until 8:00 P.M. most nights, Rick handles the evening shift on the home front—dinner, homework, baths, and bed. In addition to all of this, he also brings me coffee every Sunday morning. One weekend when he arrived, hot java in hand, he looked particularly worn out. "What's up, Rick?" I asked. "You look exhausted."

"I am," he muttered. "I worked 120 hours this pay period."

"What! You've been there a long time and your boss knows you don't want the overtime pay. I thought they knew your priority was to get home to the kids."

"They do, but last week we had some emergency overnight jobs and no one else would take them."

"What do you mean 'no one else would take them'?"

"Well, there are a lot of younger, single guys in my division, but they just cut out saying, 'No way that I'm pulling an all-nighter, even at double overtime.' I just couldn't let the company take the fall, so I went."

To my mind this is flexible policy gone too far. It would have been more fair to insist that one of the less senior workers take the overtime. Instead, Rick's company took advantage of his loyalty, knowing full well that he did not want overtime, did not need the money, and needed to be home with his children. A better solution would have required, perhaps, some creativity and negotiation with one of the other workers, and it would have been a more fair way to fill the need.

Conclusion

Since HR policies by their nature tend to be restrictive rather than expansive, creating and adjusting policies that provide for openness will be very challenging. Companies will need to try new ideas, measure them, and then retain or discard them. New ideas must not be booed down before they are thought through or given a try.

The future of HR policy, then, will require outside-the-box thinking not just in development of the policies, but on a daily basis in administering them. In order to respect the individual and entrust employees to accomplish as much as they can, policies will need an openness that allows for creative solutions. Jobs will be results, not tasks. Armed with an understanding of the skills needed, the kind of people who possess them, and what will attract these people to an employer, a company will be much better equipped to hire the best talent match. Once the hiring process has been completed, HR policies play a key role in developing commitment and ensuring employee tenure. Multiple career paths, training opportunities, scheduling flexibility, open communication, and creative benefits solutions will all play a role.

The HR professional of the future will suggest the guidelines in policy, monitor the success, and watch both fiscal and human potential results. Experimenting and changing as policies succeed and fail, the nimble HR pro will lead the way as a "strategic solutionist," finding the balance between respecting individual employee needs and priorities, and company productivity and profits.

NOTES

1. Patrick J. Sauer, "Open Door Management," *Inc.*, June 2003, p. 44.
2. "When Telecommuting Actually Works," *Business 2.0,* November 2001, p. 124.

CHAPTER 7

THE IMPACT ON RECRUITING

Friends of mine have a son, Rudy. Rudy has always been somewhat different—he is a little high strung, has trouble with social interaction, and often repeats himself. When Rudy went to school, his "difference" was given a label. (You already know how I feel about labels.) He was diagnosed with a form of autism, called Asperger's syndrome. Often bright and good with rote skills, people with this condition frequently have a narrow focus on or preoccupation with a certain subject. Rudy's passionate preoccupation was with the business of distribution. At an early age, he could recite the entire United Parcel Service schedule. He knew everywhere Federal Express flew and understood how its costing process worked. He knew the U.S. Postal Service inside and out and was able to understand its structure and how it operated.

Rudy's parents were his champions from the start. They accepted their son's differences and worked with him to make sure he had the best education possible. One day, his father was talking to a business acquaintance who was having problems in the company mailroom. It was a division of a hospital that was both spending too much on mailroom operations and having trouble getting things mailed properly. Rudy's father asked if his son might help out part-time. The friend had seen Rudy in his father's office and agreed to try him out. The role fit Rudy like a glove. Immediately the hospital saw his potential. He was able to save them money, improve effectiveness, feel productive, and make a difference. Today, you would be hard-pressed to find a mailroom that works as well, or is as cost efficient, as this one. By the way, Rudy started working while he was still in middle school. He has received promotion after promotion and is well on his way to becoming a productive adult.

THE FUTURE OF RECRUITING

Nice story, but what does it have to do with the future of recruiting? Quite simply, the story is relevant because recruiting in the future will require more one-to-one, hand-in-glove fits, such as Rudy in the mailroom. We will recruit with a focus on "fit" without limiting ourselves by labels, such as disabled, old, mother, gay, or autistic. Imagine if each person were performing a job they loved as much as Rudy loves performing his mailroom function. Imagine each employee being as competent in his job as Rudy is in his. The workplace of the future would be a great place for employer and employee alike, wouldn't it?

LESS IS MORE

Focusing on specific skills that are truly required to perform jobs will result in better matches as well as fewer closed doors for qualified candidates. Requirements such as education levels and years of experience will often become arbitrary and obsolete. In other words, by requiring less, you may gain more in terms of qualified candidates.

For example, whom do you hire: the twenty-three-year-old MBA or the seventy-three-year old with 50 years of experience? Do you pay a premium for wisdom? Wait! Maybe they're both right, but for different jobs. In the future, finding and hiring the best employees for the job will look more like a grid than a straight line. Job descriptions will need to include some honest thinking about questions such as:

Does this job require being at an office or can it be done at home?

What hours at what time of day are necessary?

For example, maybe the best brain for the job is an eighty-five-year-old who needs a nap every afternoon, but is wide-awake from 6 A.M. to 9 A.M., and maybe that will be a fine fit for your needs.

CHEMISTRY MATCH

Recruiting will need to include finding required job skills as well as matching personal chemistry to company culture. Recruiting will be the front line of offense in creating a comprehensive team that brings out the best in each member. Recruiting will need to run interference against prejudice and set the stage for objective, results-oriented management. Instead of depending on restrictive hours and rigorous policies, employers of the future will depend on creating a respectful and trusting work environment where employees will be judged by the work they do—and recruiting will lead the way.

RECRUITING: FROM ADVERSARY TO CHAMPION

Recruiting has always been a stitch in the side of company productivity. It is expensive. It is time-consuming. Even though study after study shows the high cost of employee turnover—in time, money, and lost productivity—recruiting has continued to often be rushed and superficial. When the rubber hits the road, managers often just want a warm body. Recruiters are the "bad guys" who don't get us qualified candidates, don't understand our needs, and don't fill our jobs fast enough. I am happy to report that this will not work in the future. Competition for talent and competition for profit will force companies into dramatic changes on the recruiting front.

Since hand-in-glove fit will be increasingly important, and candidates will be anything but cookie-cutter, recruiters will need to take the time to find quality employees. They will become champions of the company, the department, and the individual jobs to be filled. In addition, to find the best worker for a given job, recruiters will need to eliminate traditional stereotypes and eliminate "label barriers." Recruiters of the future will have to be champions for candidates, just as Rudy's parents were for him.

Consider Rudy's story for a moment. What if the hiring manager for the mailroom at the hospital had been approached as follows, "Hey, Jim. I have someone for your mailroom operations manager job. He's thirteen years old. He has a form of autism. He has to go to school during the day. What do you think?" It's hard to imagine that the manager would have said, "Perfect!" and signed Rudy right up!

> ### From Factory Worker to Knowledge Worker
> During the Industrial Age, the key to success lay in the system—efficiency, cost-per-unit, quotas. The success of the assembly line led to the success of the bottom line. At the same time, workers performed jobs that were repetitive and uncreative, and required skills were minimal. This is clearly no longer the case. Now, knowledge is key. Therefore, the individual becomes key. Management guru Peter F. Drucker describes knowledge workers as the major creators of wealth and jobs. Increasingly, the brainpower—i.e., the knowledge, expertise, and experience of its workers—will determine company success. In a knowledge-based company, company success depends on individual productivity, skills, and expertise. Getting the right people in the right jobs is more important than ever.

EXPAND MANAGER'S ROLE IN RECRUITING

Expanding the role of the hiring manager in the interview process can make a big difference in the quality of a new hire. According to Sally Stetson, principal and cofounder of Salveson Stetson Group, a nationally recognized executive search firm, "First, we need to return to the basics of making sure that managers know how to interview."[1] Her experience mirrors what has been described earlier in this chapter. Managers are so busy and so desperate to get a body that, instead of doing a proper quality interview using the appropriate listening and questioning skills, they are having quick conversations and making quick decisions.

With the increased importance of fit with company culture and chemistry, a quality effort of the manager is more critical than ever before.

IDEAS TO BOOST THE NEW RECRUITING EFFORT

Companies are finding new ways to improve their recruiting efforts all the time. Here is a sampling of some ideas that have proven successful:

- ❑ *Host a recruiter as a speaker.* Book a professional recruiter as the speaker for an upcoming management meeting. Insights and advice, as well as interviewing tips, can be better accepted from someone outside the company. The speakers can share their experiences about what talent is out there and what the potential candidates are looking for from an employer.

❑ *Train managers to hire their opposites.* Concepts of chemistry, comfort, trust, and respect need to be expanded to include candidates that "aren't like me." Training that broadens managers' thinking about what qualifies as "qualified," and what fits the definition of "fit," can pave the way to hiring from different generations, ethnic groups, and genders. Filling in skills that are not strengths held by the manager or others in the department can boost productivity. New insights and different opinions can improve product and process.

❑ *Interview candidates when there are no openings.* Candidates are continually sending in their resumes. Why not interview the qualified ones? Managers should be proactively interviewed in this way as well. "Unless we start turning recruiting into a proactive talent search," says Stetson, "we will continue to make mistakes in hiring."[2]

❑ *Host recruiting parties.* Make it fun and worthwhile for referral sources to recommend your company. A recruiting party can allow referral sources that may be employees, schools, professional organizations, or search firms to get to know the people and culture of your organization in a more relaxed and intimate way. Let the sources know what is new with your company, what skills are important, and what your hiring goals are. Offer incentives for qualified referrals.

❑ *Deploy roving recruiters.* Send recruiters and employee ambassadors to different venues that can be good sources of qualified candidates. These could include community centers, schools, exercise gyms, or churches. Host mini-recruiting fairs in these venues.

❑ *Go electronic—host a career choice hotline and Web site link.* For candidates interested in your company, share information about the kinds of jobs you offer and about which jobs have what requirements in terms of time, place, schedule, skills, and expected results.

❑ *Advertise*. Consider an advertising campaign that highlights the policies and benefits of working at your company. You can gear some of your recruitment efforts toward potential employees, such as the more mature worker, who may be especially attuned to what you have to offer.

JOB CANDIDATES WILL BE ABLE TO BE MORE CHOOSY

Despite recent labor conditions, projections call for a worker shortage of from 10 to 16 million peaking between 2015 and 2025, as a result of the number of available workers growing at a much lower rate than the job market.[3] As a result, employment candidates will be in the driver's seat more than ever before. You can see the pressure on recruiting beginning to build. First, the need for knowledge workers makes finding the right person for the right job more important. Then, you see the competition for those knowledge workers increase dramatically with the dwindling labor pool. Workers can, and will, be choosy and demanding. This means that companies will have to rise to the challenge in order to attract and sustain the employee base they need to succeed.

The location of the actual workplace has become a top priority for candidates. Do workers need to be in a certain place, at a certain time, in order to perform their job? More and more the answer is no. Location flexibility, therefore, can be a key asset of company recruiting.

Virtual Offices

Increasingly available, efficient, and affordable technology makes it feasible to work from anywhere, at anytime. While this can be tremendously attractive to a high-talent candidate, virtual offices can be a tough transition for old-school management that has always depended on appearances to judge worker value and contribution. This will have to change. Out of sight can no longer mean out of mind. It definitely does not mean out of service.

Telephones, computers, instant messaging, and e-mail facilitate the process of working effectively outside of the traditional office setting. Virtual offices, working from home, and even working from a coffee shop, are becoming more and more common. The workers and equipment are ready now. The mindset of management may take more time. Managers will no longer be able to depend on face-to-face interaction to feel in control.

When Workers Are Required On-Site

In certain situations and occupations, it will be necessary for workers to continue to be there, in person, to perform the jobs. First and foremost, when this is the case it must be clear up front. Applicants must know what is required of them—not only in terms of skills, but schedule and place as well—before they take a job.

The community in which a business is located also plays an important role in the success of its workers, and the attractiveness of the company. If candidates are not familiar with the area in which your company is located, highlight key places to go, things to do, and things to see. These all serve to increase the tangential, yet very real, attractiveness of your company as an employer, and they enhance employee satisfaction and tenure.

HELPING THE NEW HIRE ADJUST

Sally Stetson also makes the very valuable point that connection to the company has to be nutured after the hire. Too often, she sees that companies have not thought through the new-hire assimilation and adjustment period. As a result new employees are not fully oriented, informed, and welcomed once they come on board. In the future, where knowledge workers have been keenly recruited to find just the right fit, a smooth transition into the organization will be critical. Smooth transitions will keep new employees motivated and challenged right from the start.

❑ *Employee Buddy System.* The importance of having someone to connect with and ask questions of cannot be stressed enough. Too many times, new hires are introduced to everybody and then taken to their workstations. A best-friend or buddy program can help make sure that employees feel appreciated and supported right from the start. It sets them up with a confidante—someone who can show them the ropes beyond where the bathroom is and how to work the copier.

❑ *Thirty- and Sixty-Day Check-Ins.* Updates should be scheduled with the manager and the new employee for thirty and sixty days after the start date. These updates should be confirmed as soon as the employee starts with the company. These are not probationary reviews; they are a time for the new hire to ask questions and seek advice, check in with the manager to ask how they are doing, and for the manager to check in and ask how the company is doing at bringing the new hire up to speed and making them feel a part of the organization.

OUTSOURCED RECRUITING

I predict that by 2050 recruiting will most often be a function that is managed internally, but processed initially by outside sources. Things are already headed in that direction with the huge job databases available to both job candidates and employers. Most larger companies maintain Web sites with posted job descriptions, asking for resumes online to be stored in their database until an appropriate match can be found. However, the technology still needs to be fine-tuned in order to facilitate matching the right people to the right jobs. As it stands, these databases are still kind of hit-and-miss, spitting out thousands of candidates for each available job and hundreds of jobs for each available candidate. Candidates looking for jobs and companies looking to hire both will benefit greatly from near-future enhancement of these job recruitment databases.

❏ *Centralized Recruiting Centers.* Rather than going from interview to interview, company to company, and answering the same questions over and over, candidates will go to a central recruiting center, or even simply log in, and complete information about themselves.

❏ *Centralized Databases of Candidates.* Huge databases of job candidates, maintained by third-party database management companies, will match candidates to positions and companies almost instantly.

❏ *Centralized Databases of Companies.* In order to create the most useful database, the database management companies will collect information not only from the candidates themselves, but also from the companies and the various hiring managers in order to help match candidates to companies.

BUILDING THE DATABASE

Different types of data collected may include:

From Candidates

- ❑ Job skills
- ❑ Work experience
- ❑ Personal and professional goals
- ❑ Personal priorities at work and at home
- ❑ Background check
- ❑ Education verification
- ❑ Personality profile
- ❑ Aptitude profile
- ❑ Physical limitations

The Future: With the use of a Personal Identification Number (PIN), candidates would be able to update their profile with new educational courses, job skills, and experiences. Once modifications have been made, the account would be flagged and central database management could then verify any changes or additions.

From Managers

- ❑ 360° reviews
- ❑ Management style
- ❑ Personality profile
- ❑ Aptitude profiles
- ❑ Job skills
- ❑ Personal and professional goals

The Future: To facilitate matching a manager with employees whose skill sets compliment or even compensate for each other, data could include a manager's job skill strengths and weaknesses. For example, a manager who lacks knowledge of a certain type of software could be paired with candidates who possess that expertise.

From Companies

❑ Executive involvement

❑ Management philosophy

❑ Company profile

❑ Organizational overview

❑ Mission and vision

❑ Current financials

❑ Sample career paths

BENEFITS OF THE CENTRAL DATABASE

The increasing use of centralized candidate databases will offer a host of benefits to candidates and companies alike. These include:

❑ *Objectivity.* A central database is blind to labels and stereotypes, and can determine different elements that enhance a match without ever sharing any sensitive information with the employer. Whereas confidential data on race, religion, disability, and age can be collected, it will not need to be shared. Initial and often superficial screens such as appearance and demeanor can be eliminated when preliminary candidate matching is done through an objective central system.

❑ *Privacy.* By going through an outside third party, both companies and candidates alike can share sensitive data in confidence. Central recruiting systems also help protect candidate privacy and help facilitate career development by keeping candidates informed of ongoing matches to their developing skill sets.

This is consistent with something Sally Stetson said: The questions asked of her, as an external search consultant, are very different from the questions the candidates ask the potential employer directly. Candidates are interested in the ethics of a company and the work/life balance approaches.

❑ *Accuracy.* A central database can be maintained and updated continuously. In this way, companies will have access to an accurate talent pool of potential candidates on an on-going basis.

❑ *Timeliness.* With the pool of candidates under constant development, the length of time a position is vacant can be dramatically decreased. This saves client companies considerable time and money over developing their own candidate pools.

The virtually instantaneous nature of the centralized database is helpful to job candidates as well. How often has a candidate heard "Oh, I'm sorry. We just filled that position last week," or "We expect something to open up soon, but we're not sure when." Through centralized database recruiting systems, candidates looking for a specific type of job or a specific company receive notification, via e-mail, when such opportunities become available.

❑ *Global in Scope.* Centralized databases also eliminate geographic borders. Talent pools need not be restricted to the geographic range of "help wanted" ads. The databases will match candidates by skills, experience, and other relevant information, rather than by the fact that they "saw your ad in Sunday's paper."

This will become increasingly important, as companies will need to cast a wider net to catch the talent skills they require. For example, American students are increasingly avoiding degrees in the sciences.[4] As a result, U.S. companies requiring scientists will become more and more reliant on foreign talent. In addition, the examples described in the chapter on diversity about the increasing shortage of qualified nurses and teachers reinforce this trend of recruitment going global as we move into the future.

MORE TEMPORARY EMPLOYMENT AND PROJECT WORKERS

Temporary employment arrangements with workers can play an important role for both employers and employees in the future. Contracts for designated periods of time or for designated projects will be more frequent. These types of arrangements will allow workers to test a company's environment and compatibility, and will let employers test workers for productivity and job fit.

INCREASE INTERNS

If you don't have internships, start some. If you already do, add some. It's a great way to train, test for fit, and gain staff inexpensively. In addition to the traditional student internships, branch out and seek interns from different sources—senior homes, community centers, handicapped individuals, welfare-to-work, and people in transition. Approach ESL (English as a second language) classes, handicap centers, or summer camps. Make it fun. Pay if you can, but at least provide transportation and perhaps lunch money.

INVOLVE EMPLOYEES

Current employees can and should be an integral part of your recruiting effort. They know your company from an employee's point-of-view, so they can discuss it with job candidates in a different way from managers and human resources personnel. They probably have a good grasp of the candidate's experience, skills and abilities, so they'll recognize the right fit for your company and the potential employee.

❑ *Employees As Teachers/Trainers/Speakers.* Train employees to be teachers, tutors, and speakers. Send them out in place of recruiters to job fair events.

❑ *Employee Referrals.* Give employees incentives to refer qualified job candidates. Many companies have used this as an added recruitment tool, and it's *still* a good idea. However, repetition is key, employees forget that the incentive exists unless they are reminded through employee communications.

Employee Recruiting Focus Group

Invite a diverse group of employees, no more than twenty, to a brainstorm session and test ideas for company recruiting.

Ask questions and prompt discussion around such questions as:

1. How did you find out about this company?
2. Why were you attracted to this company?
3. What do you consider this company's best selling features?
4. What facts about our company would you stress during recruiting?
5. What would you suggest as the best way to recruit in the future? (Provide check-off boxes for job fairs, newspaper, Internet, referral, other.)

> 6. What would you change about the interview process at our company to make it more attractive?

APTITUDE TESTING WILL BE INCREASINGLY HELPFUL

Employee testing has been largely discarded in recent years, due mainly to fears of discrimination charges. Sadly, testing has been used in the past to exclude whole classes of people from rightful employment. Testing, however, can be a helpful vehicle for inclusiveness and a means to place people in jobs appropriate to their capabilities. In the future, aptitude testing will come to play an important role in the recruitment and career placement of employees. The difference will be that the employee, rather than the employer, will use test results to make choices about career direction.

While it is possible for personality to change over time, aptitudes are typically more static. Aptitudes are innate qualities with which we are born and which make us suitable for some occupations and not for others. If suitable placement of workers will be critical in the future, then aptitude must play a role.

TRAIN ONE, TRAIN ALL

To many, the processes and priorities outlined for recruiting will constitute nothing short of a revolution. In order to be successful in future recruiting, then, employers and job candidates alike will need training.

- ❑ *Candidate Training.* Individuals will need to be trained in the proper way to complete and update database information. (My mind is spinning already from contemplating the vast number of entrepreneurial coaches I expect to pop up, who will, for a modest fee, coach job candidates on how to best input data on themselves to find the best job.)

- ❑ *Hiring Manager Training.* The hiring manager will require the lion's share of the training. Senior management will need coaching and training to learn to focus on results instead of on traditional activities of measurement. Hiring managers will need interview training as well as listening training.

❑ *Human Resources Training.* HR professionals will need database training to oversee and manage the process. Orientation training will need a priority focus. Best buddy training will be needed for the new hire mentors. I will cover the subject of training in more depth in Chapter 9.

❑ *Reference Checking and Background Checking.* This is a complex subject. Many companies need a warm body right away so that background checking simply isn't completed by the start date. I know of a bank that recently found that a newly hired employee teller had an arrest and conviction record. This news was received after several months' employment during which the teller was doing a great job. Prior references had all checked out. Banks, of course, are particularly sensitive to criminal records. However, in conversation with this middle-aged mother of two, it turned out that twenty years ago she was arrested for prostitution to earn money for school. She had since turned her life around. Because this bank had the kind of human resource director who looked at the whole story and was willing to make an exception, the bank now has the kind of loyal, outstanding employee they strive to recruit.

RECRUITING AND THE FIVE TRENDS

Your company's overall recruiting effort should be revised and adapted in light of the emerging workforce trends. Following is a variety of practical recruitment ideas for you to consider in regard to each of the five trends:

IMPACT OF LONGEVITY ON RECRUITING

For the most part, the experts I interviewed are looking forward to the change in age demographics among workers. Everybody seems to know at least one anecdotal story of an older employee who does quite well and has great impact on an organization. In terms of recruiting, it is hard to picture actively recruiting in the age brackets of the 50s, 60s, 70s and beyond, but that is the future. Most employers have relaxed their retirement age and are waiving mandatory retirement. Companies are finding that the wisdom to be gained from the older worker more than compensates for any accommodations that may be required, such as flexibility in the work schedule.

❑ *Go to them.* Recruiting efforts for older workers might require going to them rather than having them come to you. A company needing, for example, consistent clerical support may recruit at an assisted living facility and find a host of ready, willing, and able workers who really would thrive earning extra money, working some limited hours, and feeling useful. They may provide a very loyal and stable mature workforce.

❑ *Make it easy to work for you.* As an alternative to going to the applicants, consider transporting applicants to your company for interviews. Have younger workers pick up older workers, or use shuttle buses, especially if public transportation is not available. Several of the policy considerations listed in Chapter 6 can be used to attract older workers.

❑ *Place ads and articles in key locations.* Companies can advertise employment opportunities and emphasize flexible schedules and other accommodations. Focus efforts to target seniors in places such as retirement communities, golf courses, and AARP/senior publications.

❑ *Host "How to Interview" seminars.* Sponsor seminars at local churches, synagogues, mosques, golf courses, and other venues to target diverse and multigenerational prospect candidates. These types of community outreach initiatives can position your company as an employer of choice.

IMPACT OF NEW HOUSEHOLD TYPES ON RECRUITING

Above all, companies need to be fully aware of the variety of new household types and the special needs or requirements that can arise.

❑ *Have specific answers ready.* New household types are becoming more apparent in recruiting as candidates are asking more pointed questions in the negotiation process such as:

❏ Can I get benefits coverage for someone who is not a legal spouse, e.g., a copartner?

❏ If I am asked to relocate, what assistance can I expect for my significant other, my ailing mother, etc.?

❏ Can I bring someone other than a spouse to company functions?

❏ *Be supportive of family needs.* Extended family is also playing an increasingly important role in the talent search. Candidates are asking about support and flexibility to care for an aging parent or a child who is disabled. This is where the flexibility required of future policies kicks in: When questions like this are handled with sensitivity, it increases a company's appeal.

❏ *Promote to different constituencies.* Target new family needs with messages of your company's work/life balance policies and benefits. This can include paid messages, by-lined articles, or nominating your company for "best places to work" awards.

❏ *Attend various support groups to describe company.* This is similar to the "roving recruiting" described earlier in this chapter. Company representatives could be employees in similar situations to the group attended, or even be members. They could attend meetings such as single-parent support groups or care-giver support groups, and provide tips and insights into how to balance work and family issues as well as describe company accommodations and flexible policies.

❏ *Provide child or elder care during interviews.* Companies can offer child or elder care for candidates during their interviews. This kind gesture would immediately position the company as respectful and supportive of family issues.

❏ *Conduct online interviews.* To make interviews as convenient as possible, companies can conduct some interviews online. Not only could static forms and applications be completed online, but actual live interviews can be conducted as well. Backstage, private chat rooms or instant messaging technology can be used to facilitate conversation.

IMPACT OF MULTIPLE GENERATIONS ON RECRUITING

The differences among the generations provide valuable insight to recruiting. For example, when seeking to woo Boomers, let them know that their experience is quite valued, that they will have extensive means for reward and recognition, and that there will be ample opportunity for new challenges and education. Let the World War II generation know that their wisdom and accomplishments are highly valued and that they will be respected for those experiences they bring to the table. Generation X'ers want to know that a work/life balance is respected and encouraged, and a guarantee that this balance will not place them on the slow track. The key in all cases, however, is that the organization must follow through on its promises.

Sally Stetson offered the following insights that are helpful to attracting talent today as well as in the future. The priorities are not common to generations, but rather to age brackets. Individual priorities are influenced by where we are in our life cycle and what is happening around us.

20-Somethings:

This group is not nearly as interested in savings plans and 401(k)s as they are about the stability of the company. They are highly sensitive to the recent spate of lay-offs accompanying the dwindling economy of the early 21st century. They also did not anticipate how hard it would be to find work, and find that they are not getting the choices they were expecting. They care very much about flexibility, vacations, time off, and a good and comfortable environment in which to work. They are also extremely interested in finding work that they feel is important and satisfying.

30-Somethings:

This group demonstrates a priority of intense work in exchange for great financial reward. Ironically, this age group also asks lots of questions about details, such as casual dress, work setting, and typical hours. They consider these types of details to be important indicators of the culture of a company. Candidates in their 30s also begin to ask how family issues are handled. They are looking for more balance and are seeking an important life outside of the office. They question the amount of hours and travel. Relocation policies are important—some want to move around while others want to be sure that they can still be on the fast track without having to move.

40-Somethings:
This group is beginning to see the future and their need for retirement savings. They are willing to risk more for some greater rewards. Work/life balance is still important. Career movement is a key motivator.

50-Somethings:
Financial security is critical for this group. Career changes are important, so that they are not bored. Retirement planning seminars are welcomed.

60+:
This group desires flexibility. They also want respect for their work experience. An important consideration for this senior group is the willingness of an organization to listen to their wisdom.[5]

- ❑ *Generation-Specific Job Fairs.* Attend or host job fairs for the specific various generations. Go beyond schools and colleges. Gear job fair presentation and company attendees to the priorities of the targeted age group.

- ❑ *Hire Along Family Lines.* Once taboo, hiring more than one person in a family can offer a company choice employees of many generations. Job skills and priorities may vary, but often the work ethic and morals will remain consistent. If one employee matches your company culture and work ethic, good chance that another family member will, too. If you have a good worker, encourage others in his or her family to apply.

Impact of Diversity on Recruiting

Great strides have been made in the areas of diversity recruitment and hiring. The ultimate goal is to have a naturally diverse workforce in which all job candidates are judged strictly on their suitability to the job.

- ❑ Conduct *online "blind" interviews.* The online interview described above can be "blind" as well as convenient. By using technology to conduct a live interview without being face-to-face with the candidate, skills and job fit can be more objectively assessed.

❑ *Publish competency profiles.* For each job, a competency profile lists those skills necessary to perform it. The profile should emphasize the results expected of the person performing the job. In addition, it can include everything from specific skills and knowledge requirements such as computer languages, to training available, to where the job is located and what hours are required. Physical demands such as heavy lifting, long-time standing or sitting, driving, or travel can be listed. These profiles should be easily accessible through the company Web site, printable in large, normal typeface. Braille, video, or audio versions can be produced as well.

❑ *Proactively recruit "not like me."* Companies can recognize and reward men recruiting women, whites recruiting minorities, young recruiting old.

❑ *Publish diversity statistics of employee base.* Just as colleges publish the demographics of their student-base and programs aimed at diversity, companies can do the same. Include this information in both company brochures and on the Web site.

❑ *Reach out to handicapped residential communities, training facilities, and schools.* Just as companies can "go to them" to attract and recruit more mature workers, you can reach out, offsite, to attract and recruit handicapped workers.

Impact of Trust, Respect, and Ethics on Recruiting

Companies will have to be more attuned to the increased interest in trust, respect, and ethics. More and more, this will mean demonstrating to potential employees that your company fosters an enlightened workplace and supports and encourages social responsibility.

❑ *Be aware of the importance of company reputation.* Workers of the future will demand an ethical employer where they can flourish in an environment of trust and respect. No matter how I sliced, diced, and categorized the demographics in the first half of the book, this major common theme was clear. As such, company reputation will mean even more in the recruiting process of the future. Workers want to be proud of their company and feel that they are respected for their contributions.

❑ *Send employee ambassadors.* Whether to college campuses or job fairs, don't just send representatives from human resources, send employee ambassadors. Choose workers who are warm and enthusiastic about the company, who represent the type of worker you want to attract. Also choose ambassadors of different generations, cultures, and ethnic groups.

❑ *Prove company worthiness.* Recruiters of the future will be required to prove that an environment of trust and respect exists in order to attract the talent they desire. Key to this will be the flexibility of the policies as candidates negotiate their work agreement. Cookie-cutter benefits, schedules, and work arrangements will be out the window. Future employees will demand not just that their employer put its money where its mouth is—they will demand that their company put its policies there as well.

❑ *Publish your benefits policy.* Whatever benefits and policies your company develops that shows the importance and priority of individual trust and respect, share them! It could be in the form of a separate brochure used as a recruiting tool.

❑ *Share worker testimonials.* Videos or CD-ROMs showing the company on an average day, with employees making statements about the benefits, culture, openness, and flexibility of the company, can help expand upon the words of recruiters and attract key candidates.

❑ *Allow candidates to interview with a client or employee.* After human resources and the manager have met a candidate they feel comfortable with, give the candidate an opportunity to speak with a client of the company and/or with a potential coworker. This need not be a formal interview, per se, but instead it could provide the candidate with a chance to get to know the company better and specifically gain insight about company integrity.

❑ *Expand recruiting materials.* Include ethics policy, charity, and philanthropic work of the company in recruiting material that is posted on the Web, shown on videos, printed in brochures, sent and displayed to potential candidates.

❑ *Keep employee alumni in the loop.* Share company information with good former employees to keep them in the spirit of the organization and potentially interested in coming back.

❑ *Begin recruiting-related community service.* Your company can plug into the state or local welfare-to-work programs as a source of job candidates. Another community service that can help build a qualified employee pool would be to provide training on basic reading, writing, math, and/or computer skills. Or you may want to consider implementing an afternoon program for youth that includes training/education and leads to internships or a potential employment opportunity, if they qualify.

Testing Issues

When part of your company recruiting process includes testing, make sure the testing is truly relevant and required to find qualified candidates. If it is, then be sensitive to several issues.

◆ Large print and/or loud volume versions may be needed for older applicants

◆ Word choice and jargon may inadvertently exclude certain cultures

◆ Different language versions may be needed

◆ Braille, video, or audio versions may be needed

◆ Gear samples and examples to different cultures

◆ Be sensitive to cultural differences that may offend

◆ Consider offering the test in both written and oral formats

---

❑ *Redesign jobs according to the talent that's available.* What appears to be a lack of qualified candidates could just be a faulty or narrow assignment of skills on your part. Companies can break up jobs in different ways to accommodate different types of workers. Break up input from analysis. Separate research from sales calling. Divide job duties into different day parts. For example, instead of having one person work a job all day, consider breaking up a work load such that a senior works early morning, a parent works during school hours, and a Nexter works at night.

Recruiting in 2015: How the Process Might Work

Step 1: Digital Matching

- ❏ The company provides a description of requirements for a job opening.
- ❏ A regression analysis of job requirements and the candidate database provides a list of possible candidates which expect to mesh with the company at many levels, including culture, ethics, job skills, scheduling priorities, and work/life priorities.
- ❏ Testing is processed and recorded.
- ❏ Creation of a talent pool database provides on-going support and saves companies time and money.

Step 2: Virtual Introductions

- ❏ The hiring company performs a video review of top candidate matches provided by the recruitment database management company. Tapes have been created previously as part of the development of the database.
- ❏ Top candidates view a videotape, DVD, and/or print information about the potential employer, provided by the recruitment database management company. Tapes and company information are provided to the recruitment database management company when the hiring company becomes a client.

Step 3: Teams, Tours, and Trials

- ❏ Selected top candidates are interviewed and meet not only the manager, but also potential coworkers.

❏ Top candidates receive a comprehensive tour of the company.

❏ A narrowing field of top candidates spends a "day in the life" at their new possible employer.

Step 4: Top Candidates and Hiring Management Roundtable

❏ A customized work relationship package is negotiated through a menu of options for new hires. Reference and background checks are automatically performed.

Step 5: New Hire Orientation and Transition Management

❏ The selected candidate joins the company and receives a comprehensive orientation, any necessary on-the-job training, and a buddy/mentor to help guide the transition to the new company. The manager provides a comprehensive list of goals: expected results and timelines.

❏ A ninety-day review is a two-way exchange of results versus goals, training needs, questions about systems, policies, etc., and suggestions for improvement.

CONCLUSION

Recruiting will assume a new and revitalized role in the future. No longer a process that just screens resumes and reacts to the urgent need to fill a job, recruitment will be a strategic function that champions company culture as well as employee individuality.

Those responsible for recruiting will need to be at the highest level within the organization and to be deeply involved in corporate strategy, corporate culture, and corporate philosophies. Outsourcing to a centralized database of candidates will help keep ahead of the curve with a talent pool that is sharp and readily available.

Recruitment will be the catalyst that not only blends all age groups and types of people into the employee base, but also insists that the organization back up the claims of the recruiter in terms of corporate culture and beliefs. Trust and respect will not be mere lip service, but indeed will be the culture and belief system of the corporation. Whether the employer is a small entrepreneurial firm or a large corporation, the same principles will apply to recruiting.

NOTES

1. Sally Stetson, interview, July 2003.
2. Ibid.
3. Lindy Williams and Jeff Brown, *The 21st Century Workforce: Implications for Human Resources in the 21st Century* (Hoboken, N.J.: John Wiley & Sons, 2003).
4. Jeffrey Mervis, "Down for The Count?" *Science*, May 16, 2003, p.1,070.
5. Sally Stetson, interview, July 2003.

CHAPTER 8

THE IMPACT ON COMPENSATION AND BENEFITS

Of all the aspects of human resources, perhaps none will be more dramatically affected by the trends of the future than compensation and benefits.

The subject of pay and benefits is very complex. In light of the trends we have discussed, the design of benefit plans will change drastically in the future. No single set of benefits will be successful for all employees. Furthermore, benefits will represent a larger and larger share of the total cost of an employee. Compensation, on the other hand, will remain an important element of what attracts and keeps the right people.

In the future, flexibility will once again be the operative mindset in terms of both compensation and benefits. Creating a total-rewards package of pay and benefits that reflects the needs, desires, and priorities of individual employees will make a company more attractive to key talent in the workforce.

Consider the story of Kathy Davis, chief operating officer of CGI. Kathy has two children from her first marriage, and is a single mother head of household. When her children were quite young, they were diagnosed with a genetic condition called Stargardt's Disease (a form of macular degeneration); quite simply, that means that they are legally blind. Her little girl was diagnosed at age six, then her little boy, two years younger than his sister, contracted the disease one year later. This single woman received no child support from the children's father.

Kathy joined CGI prior to her children's diagnosis. We were able to support her benefits and compensation needs in many ways as she worked through the various challenges that life threw her way. Salary was most important to her as she dealt with her children with special needs. Medical benefits trumped cash needs when her children became disabled. Not only was diagnosis and treatment needed, but both children also had more than average number of accidents due to sight impairment. Later, she needed to recover savings and pay for her two children to go to college, with special needs to accommodate their disability. Throughout the course of her employment with CGI, Kathy has always provided above-average results to compensate for the flexibility required in her compensation, benefits, and work schedule.

The workforce of the future, as we know, will be many more Kathys and many fewer "Ozzies" with Harriet at home with the two kids and the dog. Benefits and compensation will need to change with the times.

Start with a Total-Rewards Strategy

In developing effective compensation and benefits for the future, strategy is the most important starting place. More than ever before, the complex workforce of the future will require that a company think through a human resource strategy and allow that strategy to guide decisions.

Each year as budget time approaches, management performs the "dance of the dollars." They seek the delicate balance among profit margins, cost increases, supply, demand, and a myriad of decisions accompanying these factors. Human resources is no small chunk of the costs. Salaries and benefits have traditionally ranked first and second in size of costs for many companies. Add to the mix:

❑ The cost of living index increase affecting employees.

❑ An enormous medical cost increase (three times the cost of living over the next ten years).

❑ A longer living work force that most likely has not saved as much as they should. Fifty percent of employees who leave a company take their 401(k) and spend it instead of rolling it over for their future.

With so many challenges facing the total-rewards program, a strong strategy that considers company philosophy, priorities, and productivity into the future can make decision making about compensation and benefits, or total rewards, a great deal easier.

SAMPLE STRATEGY 1: HIGH TURNOVER IS OKAY

One possible HR strategy may be to decide that high turnover is acceptable, or even desirable, among certain ranks of employees. As a result, employers might place a priority on creating an effective process to facilitate replacement and on keeping operating processes clear and streamlined. In addition, pay for these employees is average and benefits paid for by the company are minimal.

With this strategy in place, it is not a difficult decision, when a 16-percent renewal increase comes along on the medical plan, to simply pass it along to your employees. Perhaps, instead, you increase the deductible for your employees and add the option of a Health Savings Account (HSA) paid into by employees to help future medical needs. If some employees reach a point where they feel the cost of their medical benefits is too high at your company, they can seek employment elsewhere—and you're ready to replace them. You might have a different strategy for your senior people, supervisors, and management staff where high turnover is not acceptable. After careful design and discrimination testing is performed, creative strategies can work.

SAMPLE STRATEGY 2: BENEFITS AS A COMPETITIVE ADVANTAGE

A different strategy can be that benefits, particularly the medical plan, become the crown jewel of the company retention program, and that strategy guides every decision made relative to compensation and benefits. Employees must feel they have the best health insurance possible. So, instead of tinkering with co-pays and deductibles each year, the company absorbs the bulk of the cost increase. A clear strategy, set in place in order to retain key talent, guides the decision. The strategy is designed to increase profitability to pay for this jewel.

These two sample strategies are at different ends of the benefits spectrum. There are as many possible strategies as there are companies. Each company needs to gather its best thinkers to consider various strategies and to determine what total-rewards strategy will best serve in the face of the emerging workforce. With HR strategy in place, decisions around compensation and benefits will not be a walk in the park, but each company will at least have a compass. Regardless of the strategy chosen, however, clear communication and education about benefits as a significant part of total compensation will be important.

COMPENSATION

When I started in the field of human resources over thirty years ago, compensation was clearly king. In those days most people stated that they worked to get paid. I know I did. Benefits were fairly standard across the board and represented about 10 to 20 percent additional compensation above salary.

> ### The "Good Old Days" of Compensation Design
> One of my earliest jobs was at a large insurance company where I was responsible for preparing job descriptions and evaluating the jobs by a point factor system. I learned a complicated process to evaluate relative job value based on the complexity of the tasks performed and proximity to management level. At this particular company, the impact of my job became obvious early on. Believing that salesmanship and favors would literally earn them "points," coworkers began courting me. By letting me know how important they were, each hoped that at evaluation time, I would find his (and I do mean *his*) job worthy of the 2300-point minimum necessary to be admitted to the executive dining room. If I found a job to be worth enough points, many other perks came to the executives, such as membership in the country club, which included weekend golf games with the family and the boss. My entire job seemed to revolve around making sure I was not bribed, so I could fairly evaluate job descriptions. My how times have changed! Very few compa-

nies still use a point system like that, very few have those kinds of rewards anymore, and most companies use a market-based payment system.

THE DIMINISHING ROLE OF PAY

While still an important factor in attracting and retaining employees, pay is not the be all and end all that it once was. Since the late 1990s, compensation has been playing a diminishing role in what drives employees. We are now primarily an information and service economy. Today, more companies thrive thanks to knowledge workers than factory workers. Even manufacturing jobs today require decision making, creativity, and interaction with others. As such, systems of recognition and reward beyond pay become increasingly important because jobs seem much more integrally tied to our self-perception and our self-esteem. Another factor in the diminishing role of pay is that we are essentially making less, so other things need to fill in. Companies are not awarding the big raises that were once common. An article in *The Economist*[1] in February 2002 reported that at three-quarters of American companies, pay is remaining flat, and at one out of twenty companies, pay is actually declining. When I began in the compensation field in the 1970s, annual raises ranging from 8 to 12 percent were common. By the year 2000, most annual salary budgets were either capped or limited to a 3-percent increase across the entire employee base. Spurred on by both tight budgets and employee desires, companies are increasingly looking for effective rewards beyond money.

The Power of Rewards

We had an interesting first-hand encounter with the power of nonfinancial rewards. One year, the employees at CGI had worked diligently and effectively through a particularly grueling fall season of our clients' benefits renewals. We wanted to do something special for them. After a lively discourse about money versus other rewards, we decided to do both: Each employee would receive a $500 bonus, and we would close the company for a day. The employees' reactions to the two forms of recognition were remarkable. The distribution of the $500 bonuses was met with a sincere "thank you," but when we announced that the company would be closed the day after Thanksgiving for the first time in our history, the announcement was met with a rousing cheer! Had I done all my book research prior to this experience, I might not have been so shocked by this reaction.

THE "ETHICAL PERFECT STORM"

According to Ted Buyniski, a principal of Mellon Human Resources and Investors Solutions, compensation has had a stunning setback due to an "ethical perfect storm." Buyniski says that several factors have contributed to the decline in business ethics. For years, the stock market was more than a bull market—it was a cash cow. Executives were chasing the almighty dollar when the bubble burst in 2000. Many were financially wiped out. Complex and convoluted business laws attracted executives with loopholes large enough to drive their debt through, allowing them to keep up appearances and promises to stockholders. Then came Enron, Tyco, and other corporate scandals—and the house of cards fell. In addition, the exposure of illegal practices by mutual fund companies rocked the business world again.

The pendulum has now started to swing in the other direction. Here are some of the "new" ideas being tried in compensation:

❑ *Set corporate-wide fair pay levels.* As a result of legislative reactions, the stock exchange correction, and more government intervention in the executive suite, there is now an increasing effort to do things ethically. One result is a growing effort to set fair and equitable pay levels throughout the organization.

❑ *Make money the old-fashioned way, earn it.* There have been stories of salespeople who are paid on *booked* orders getting customers to sign up orders they don't really need so the salespeople can be paid a bonus, only to have the order rescinded before it is ever shipped. This kind of unscrupulous practice is now diminishing. The future focus is on honesty in accounting for revenues and expenses and on customer satisfaction. Companies are looking for measures that are the least susceptible to cheating, games, and loopholes and that are the most advantageous to long-term relationships.

❑ *Look at the big picture to find what's fair and ethical.* Buyniski tells of one company that had traditionally based bonuses purely on financial measures. As a result, the company once paid out bonuses and laid off 10 percent of the workforce in the same year. The following year, although they made their numbers, the CEO went to the board of directors and recommended that no bonuses be paid, in order to save jobs. This represents a seismic shift from the time when executives would often increase their own bonuses by laying off workers, without ever feeling that this was somehow irresponsible. Executives are now looking at how their own compensation works and how they pay their people. The ethical imperative has more impact on pay than ever before.

CAFETERIA COMPENSATION

Keeping in mind the picture of the emerging workforce of our future, we need a new approach to compensation. At different points of life and in different personal situations, an individual is willing to take different risks, has different priorities, and desires different rewards from their work. Compensation in the future should be flexible and adaptable enough to allow workers the opportunity to choose from a menu of compensation choices including:

❑ Base pay

❑ Incentive pay

❑ Company stock

❑ Time

❑ *Allow employees to craft their own compensation package.* "Companies can structure pay that opens or closes potential employee pools," says Buyniski.[2] A growing number of companies are allowing their employees to create their own compensation package. Employees can trade off among the various elements of pay. This will encourage loyalty and reinforce the priority of individual respect.

The following comparison shows how, in Buyniski's view, employees in different age brackets might choose among the compensation options:

Employees	Compensation Priorities
In their 20s	Exchange pay for equity
In their 30s and 40s	Have a standard compensation and benefit program
In their 50s and 60s	Cut back on base salary, design an incentive plan

This type of system becomes a compensation plan of choice. Those willing to take a risk on the success of the company would get $1.40 instead of $1.00 if certain "at risk" goals are met. This is the equivalent of a 40-percent load for putting pay at risk. Perhaps a company could, for example, compensate a person $2.00 compared to $1.00 + stock for those who take stock in lieu of pay. Or, some employees may earn 10 percent more pay if they take deferred compensation. Within limits you can model out best and worst case scenarios and educate employees to make good financial decisions.[3]

❑ *Make choices clear and provide guidance.* As long as employees receive a clear explanation of their options and guidance to make good decisions, cafeteria compensation will recognize and respect the individual employee. The challenge of cafeteria compensation is that administration will be difficult. In addition, employees will need extensive education in the pros and cons of various options and protection from making bad decisions.

❑ *Match pay structure to target employees.* Structuring pay to match the demographics of the type of candidates you seek allows compensation to play a role in recruiting in a new way, different from the traditional "just offer more money" approach.

❑ *Give employees annual compensation "checkups."* There might be a new HR function that helps individual employees plan their careers and compensation choices with yearly checkups. This could be a major retention tool for companies that need highly skilled employees and want low turnover.

BENEFITS

Now let's turn our focus to how the emerging workforce will demand changes in benefits. Without a doubt, the biggest challenges facing employers, and even our country at large, are health care and retirement.

HEALTH CARE

The skyrocketing costs of health care are on the forefront of concern for consumers, businesses, and the government. Here is another way to consider the increasing cost of health care, by looking at the increasing cost of medical coverage as a percentage of salary (Figure 8-1).

With the realistic assumptions of 3 percent annual salary increases and 9 percent annual medical coverage cost increases, in twenty years, single medical coverage will cost more than 30 percent of salary and family medical coverage will cost nearly 90 percent of salary.

Why Rising Medical Costs Aren't Really News

The cost of health care will increase three times as fast as the rest of the economy. As much as this seems like big news, it should not be. Consider that in 1962, the monthly cost of health-care coverage was about $7.50 per month for single coverage and $20.00 per month for family coverage. In 2002, health-care coverage was about $275 per month for single coverage and about $775 per month for family coverage. This works out to a compound rate of growth of 9.5 percent annually.

Two observations are relevant here. First, health care is a constantly growing package of goods and services. A new drug, test, or procedure is announced nearly every day, and we are assertive in demanding it. Second, as health care makes us live longer in good health, the cost of health care goes up, not down, because we have more years to use the drugs, tests, and procedures. In light of these two observations, one could conclude that costs for health care are so much higher because health care is so much better.

Figure 8-1. Forecasting cost of medical care as percentage of salary.

	Salary Increase (3%)	Medical Increase (6%)		Medical Increase (9%)	
		Single	Family	Single	Family
Today	$35,000	$3,500	$10,000	$3,500	$10,000
Percentage of pay		(10%)	(29%)	(10%)	(29%)
In 10 Years	$47,000	$6,300	$17,900	$8,300	$23,700
Percentage of pay		(13%)	(38%)	(18%)	(50%)
In 20 Years	$63,000	$11,200	$32,000	$19,600	$56,000
Percentage of pay		(18%)	(51%)	(31%)	(89%)

Case in Point: Alex's Growing Family Longevity

My business partner, Alex, drew up an interesting chart about his own family that highlights its increasing longevity. Alex's chart (Figure 8-2) lets us see clearly that advances in health care have lengthened our lives.

Alex, who is not yet 65, does have high cholesterol, but it is managed with medication. An avid mountain bike rider, he need not limit his exercise, much to his relief.

My father was another terrific example of increasing longevity and vitality. He lived on his own and contributed productively to society into his 90s, tooling around in his new car. After a sixty-year career as an attorney, he then volunteered on the bench as a special master (a lawyer asked to work as a judge to clear the court system) for another ten years. Once again, advances in health care allowed him to live a long and vital life.

How to Pay for the New Technology and Drugs

This is a topic for another entire book, but suffice it to say, guided by a strong strategy, it is not such a dismal situation. In short, however, consider some good news: By living longer and in better health, which is facilitated by the new technology and drugs, we can work productively for more years and therefore help pay for the increased health-care costs, which are a result of the new technology and drugs.

Figure 8-2. Alex's family health changes.

Age at Death	Alex's Family Member	Years Lived with Limited Ability	Medical Conditions/ How Managed
50	Grandfather	0	None: died of a heart attack in his shop
60	Grandmother	10 Years	Heart "condition" / heart attacks Managed with pain medication Finally an oxygen tent
82	Father (a doctor)	40 Years	Arterial sclerosis (cholesterol) Managed through diet and nitroglycerine Early heart medicines in his later years Restricted exercise

The Controversial Genetics Card

In the coming years, we will all be faced with new ideas surrounding medical costs. Whatever your company strategy, employees will be questioning not only what to do morally and ethically, but how to pay for it. Genetics will increasingly play a role.

Genetic research gives individuals and families valuable information that allows them to make informed decisions relative to inherited health issues. While the cost of genetic testing and counseling is incurred up front, the early detection and possible correction of certain health problems will save both lives and money in the long run.

❑ *Keep the information private.* While legislation is most likely forthcoming that will prohibit using genetic information in business, hiring, or health-care coverage decisions, companies can be proactive in creating privacy policies relative to genetic testing and its results.

❏ *Subsidize and support individual decisions.* As genetic testing becomes more common, some employees will feel a "need to know"
their predisposition toward certain medical conditions. I have a
friend who had a family history of death due to breast cancer, and
she chose to have genetic testing to see if she had the gene. She
did. She chose radical, preemptive breast removal. Employees making these kinds of decisions will need financial as well as emotional
support from their employers.

On the other hand, even when genetic predisposition seems
likely, some employees don't want genetics tests. Employers must
be open to and supportive of that decision as well.

My Own Bout with Genetics

One day, not too long ago, I was reading an article that described several
genetic factors that increase a woman's chance of developing breast cancer.[4] There were three "risk" factors: 1) a familial history of breast cancer,
2) an Ashkenazi-Jewish heritage, and 3) a late first pregnancy. To me, this
represented the triple threat—I had all three.

I had long known of the history of breast cancer in my family. Both
my mother and maternal aunt developed breast cancer. As a result, I have
always been conscientious in diet and exercise, as well as in getting regular
check-ups. When I read about these other risk factors, though, I started
worrying all over again. Should I get the genetic test to see if I have the
breast cancer gene? At my next check-up, I asked my doctor. "What do *you*
think?" she asked, turning the question back to me.

"Well," I replied slowly, "I'm not sure what I would do if I had the
test. I already watch my diet, exercise, and get regular check-ups. The only
other option, if I found I had the gene, would be to get preemptive surgery,
which I don't want to do. So I guess genetic testing would only make me
worry more."

"Exactly," she answered. "In my view, genetic testing can be very helpful if it can give you insight that guides important decisions. On the other
hand, if getting the test wouldn't change your behavior or guide any decisions, I would not recommend it."

I felt so much better. I have chosen to just stay the course of taking
care of myself, without pursuing genetic testing.

Genetic testing, as much as it is growing rapidly in ease and cost-effectiveness, is still in its infancy. It tests for some diseases, but not all. It provides advance insights into diseases that have no solutions. By 2050, it will be commonplace. By then, there may be a pill that prevents breast cancer as simple as the one for cholesterol. As genetic testing matures to its full promise, we will have to figure out its highest and most ethical use. I believe that long-term it will save both lives and health-care dollars.

New Tactical Ideas

Three acronyms describe a relatively new tactic to reduce the rate of increase in health-care costs.

Consumer Directed Health Care	(CDHC)
Health Reimbursement Accounts	(HRAs)
Health Saving Arrangements	(HSAs)

Consumer Directed Health Care (CDHC) is a plan design alternative to traditional HMO, PPO, or Indemnity plans. These plans are typically quite generous in their coverage and require relatively small payments by the employee or family member at claim time. The CDHC model exposes the employee to a large initial deductible (often $1,000 or more).

The Health Reimbursement Account (HRA) is an employer-provided line of credit that the employee may use to offset all or part of the large CDHC deductible. Unused portions of the HRA may be carried forward to future plan years.

The combination of CDHC and HRA offer the possibility that employees will modify their behavior about medical expenses since part of the claim cost will be coming out of their HRA (or even worse, out of their pocket). When combined with user-friendly information tools, the hope is that employees will become sophisticated buyers of medical care cost and that in the process the rate of cost increases will be less.

Health Saving Arrangements (HSAs) are a newer vehicle that offers even greater attraction to employees and therefore should increase their willingness to select CDHCs. HSAs can be funded with both employer and employee contributions, they enjoy generous income tax benefits, and they are fully vested and portable.

Although regulations are still needed, HSAs promise to make CDHC plans more attractive and therefore to help further to reduce the rate of health-care cost increases.

Retirement/Pension

As much as skyrocketing health care costs are the number one dilemma keeping human resource professionals up at night today, I contend that there is an impending retirement crisis that will be as great if not an even greater challenge.

Pensions or 401(k)s

According to *U.S. News and World Report* in December 2001, only about 20 million workers were still covered by a traditional defined-benefit pension plan.[5] Self-directed defined-contribution plans, such as 401(k)s, were covering more than 55 million employees. The number of traditional pension plans is decreasing due to costs, employees' desire for a portable and visible account balance, and government mandates that have made the implementation of pension plans extremely complex. The question is whether a traditional fixed benefit pension system is preferable to today's increasingly popular employee-directed retirement saving plans, such as 401(k)s. Some are uneasy about self-directed retirement accounts, saying investment losses and 401(k) government limitations demonstrate a need for something more dependable. Further, as Karen Ferguson, the director of the Pension Rights Center in Washington, D.C., cautions, even though programs such as 401(k)s are increasingly popular, half of the workers in the private sector have no company retirement plans at all. This is the biggest challenge. Americans aren't saving enough. The median retirement savings of the Baby Boomer generation is only $40,000. The Government likely will come up with more programs to encourage and support adequate retirement savings, and companies will no doubt become involved in implementing some of these programs. However, a crisis looms and there is no cure on the immediate horizon.

How Much Do You Need to Retire?
Here is a little quiz I like to give when I speak to a group of students. Play along and see where your answers take you.

Question 1: To what age do you expect to live?

Question 2: At what age do you want to retire?

Question 3: At today's rate, how much money do you want to have for each year of your retirement?

Now, take your answer to question 2 and subtract it from your answer to question 1. Then, multiply that answer by your answer to question 3. How much money will you need to have in order to retire? Just for fun, subtract the amount you currently have saved toward retirement from this total. Take that net amount and divide it by the difference between your current age and your answer to question 2. That is how much you need to save each year until your retirement. How are you doing toward your retirement goal? If you are like most people I share this quiz with, your answers to the three questions are optimistic and the resulting amount of money you will need to retire is overwhelming. That is the heart of today's retirement crisis.

Getting Employees to Save

According to a January 2002 article in *The Wall Street Journal*, Americans save only 1 percent of their disposable personal income, down from 9 percent ten years earlier.[6] As the retirement savings quiz indicates, most households in the United States are drastically unprepared for a financially comfortable retirement. Furthermore, neither employers nor employees are currently undertaking the steps necessary to avoid this pending crisis.

"Save More Tomorrow" Plan

Richard Faler, an economist at the University of Chicago Business School, has a plan that he believes will help the "notorious low savers" of America. He calls it "Save More Tomorrow," an idea he developed with Economics Professor Shlomo Benartzi from the Anderson School at the University of California in Los Angeles. The concept involves employees permitting their employers to channel a large amount of any future salary increases into retirement plans. Dr. Faler feels that most people would agree in advance to channel pay raises to savings because it does not involve present income. In a test program in one small firm, savings rates for participating employees jumped from less than 4 percent to almost 12 percent in only twenty-eight months. On the down side, however, only 782 out of 5,000 potential employees signed up for the plan.

One Way NOT to Go: Robbing Peter to Pay Paul
Wal-Mart stores, according to *The Wall Street Journal* of February 5, 2002, offered to permit workers to use their 401(k) retirement plan funds to offset a 30 percent increase in health insurance costs charged by the company beginning in January 2002.[7] Workers were shocked and many believed they had no choice but to rob their retirement nest eggs to pay for their health coverage. Some who could not afford the new rates dropped their important health and dental coverage altogether.

Phased Retirement

Phased retirement is the term used to describe a gradual decrease in the number of hours worked each week and the amount of pay received. This often takes place over many years. With phased retirement employees can continue to give to and gain from their organizations, and not become stagnant. According to Helen Darling of the National Business Group on Health, many companies recognize a need to encourage phased retirement in order to retain skilled and experienced employees.

Postponing Retirement

As we've already discussed in regard to longevity, older Americans feel more vital and more interested in working past age 65. This helps reduce the strain on the overall retirement system, as well as on an individual and a company basis.

By working longer, employees will help companies' productivity and profitability and, at the same time, create more money to pay for health care. The emerging workforce, then, brings its own solution to today's biggest challenges of health care and retirement. Although by living longer we may require more health care, we will, at the same time, stay active and productive members of society longer. The longer we stay working, active, and productive, the longer we are helping pay for both health care and retirement.

The following illustrates the advantage of a current twenty-five-year-old working to age 75 instead of age 65:

Let's assume a bright and ambitious young person enters the work force at age 25, earns a starting yearly salary of $30,000, does a good job, and receives yearly raises of 3 percent. Forty years later, still full of vim and vigor, this person, who is now middle-aged, agrees to work ten more years. This person's employer gratefully accepts the decision, as workers, especially ones who already possess the experience and skills to do the specific job, are increasingly hard to find.

Here's what happens:

Age	Annual Salary	Employee/Employer FICA*
65	$ 97,861	$14,972
66	$100,797	$15,421
67	$103,821	$15,884
68	$106,936	$16,360
69	$110,144	$16,360
70	$113,448	$17,357
71	$116,851	$17,877
72	$120,357	$18,414
73	$123,968	$18,966
74	$127,687	$19,535
TOTAL	$1,121,870	$171,637

*7.65 percent contributed by each.

The worker earns $1,121,870 more than if he or she retired at age 65. Between spending, taxes, and additional retirement savings, eventually the whole amount will circulate back into the economy. At age 75, when the worker finally retires, the retirement savings will have increased by ten more years of investments and, more important, ten more years of investment return. Plus, the worker's retirement account, social security, and Medicare will be less strained because the worker is likely to be drawing down benefits for a shorter period of time, say twenty years (age 75 to 95) rather than thirty years (65 to 95).

The employer will benefit from a competent, experienced worker's willingness and ability to work an additional ten productive years since this will help the employer stay fully staffed in a period of declining younger population.

Wait, There's More!

Before you throw this book out the window for suggesting that we all work ten years longer, consider:

- ❏ Most of us will not want to just sit around at age 65. We will be too young to retire.
- ❏ Working longer offers us choices and opportunities to pursue "dream jobs" and to reinvent ourselves.
- ❏ The whole paradigm of work is shifting—away from "9 to 5" and even further away from "7 A.M. to 7 P.M." More flexibility in both time and place of work will become the norm.

Total Rewards

Total rewards will be the compensation and benefits package of the future. This will envelope both the traditional factors of pay and benefits, as well as other forms of "compensation," such as time, work place, training, and education.

The Key Is Flexibility

The recurrent theme of this book has been future flexibility and focus on the individual. Nowhere will this be more apparent than in the development of total-rewards packages for employees. The future will hold a menu of money, responsibilities, learning, benefits, and time.

Beyond Pay and Benefits

Several of the ideas for employee-friendly policies presented in Chapter 6 can enhance the total rewards of an organization. Just to review a few:

❏ A cafeteria that prepares healthy foods to take home and heat up when you get there

❏ A concierge service that purchases and wraps presents, picks up milk and bread, or drops off clothing at the dry cleaners

❏ A fitness program custom-developed for employees and designated funding

❏ A nutritionist on staff to customize diet and educate about food choice

❏ Driver services to pick up kids, parents, or handicapped family members, or to take employees to the doctor

The more ways in which employees feel they are being rewarded by your company, the better they feel about working for you. One of the goals of the total-rewards concept is to make employees actively look forward to going to work. This is a counterbalance to the trend where people want more time off and more ability to be home.

Other Ideas for Enhancing Total Rewards

Here are some additional ideas employers can try to augment their compensation and benefits packages:

❏ *Financial Education.* This harkens back to the financial planning assistance suggested earlier, as well as the annual compensation package check-ups. Companies can offer experts and provide information to help employees understand how much money they really need and how much to put away each year. Employees also need continuing education about the stock market, household budgeting, and savings options.

❏ *Total-Rewards Coach.* Companies can make available a "coach" who works one on one with employees to educate and advise them through the process of putting together their total-rewards package.

❏ *Computer Modules.* Software can be made available for computer models of financial planning, savings options education, or retirement planning. These would allow for individualized solutions, privacy, and an opportunity for employees to test different scenarios.

❑ *Center of Excellence for Health Care.* If an employee or an unemployed member of their designated family wants to go to the "best" health care facility in the world for a certain condition, the company can offer counseling, travel compensation, or special work arrangements.

❑ *Advocacy Help.* When an employee or a family member is facing a complex medical situation or hospital stay, the company can provide an advocate to sit in on doctor meetings, take notes, participate in discussions, and even fight for the right care.

❑ *Group Purchase Power.* Organize and leverage group purchase power on behalf of employees for items such as food, tickets, travel, electronics, and home goods.

Total Rewards and the Five Trends

In the near future, companies will have to construct their compensation and benefits packages with an eye toward the five emerging workforce trends. Let's take a look at some ideas that can help match your total-rewards program to your employees' needs and keep the company's costs in line as well.

Total Rewards Related to Longevity

❑ *Enhance retirement savings flexibility.* Companies can allow employees to add to their retirement savings even after they retire. At the same time, companies can allow employees to delay taking money out of their retirement plan, so it can grow. Companies can continue to lobby the government for the best tax treatment.

❑ *Offer extra financial help for prescriptions.* Set up a company-sponsored fund for help with the cost of prescriptions not covered by health-care insurance or Medicare.

❑ *Offer reverse mortgages.* For older employees who have paid off their house but are on limited income, reverse mortgages can be attractive. These home loans allow the homeowner to turn a portion of their equity into cash, with no repayment required until the house is sold. Companies may offer reverse mortgages through a third-party vendor, or provide education and application assistance to their employees.

❏ *Offer reverse life insurance.* Allow older employees to use a portion of their paid-for life insurance now rather than holding it all for a beneficiary.

❏ *Create company housing.* Create company-sponsored housing. A multigenerational facility would encourage community among employees and allow them to support each other.

Creating a Whole Town

In Eagleview, Pennsylvania, a real-estate developer created townhouses for lower income employees, single-family homes for middle income employees, and even some mansions. They also built a nursing home, a gym, a day care center, a series of retail stores, three restaurants, and a town square with planned social events. Finally, this planned community has a corporate center. The concept was to create an old-fashioned town where you work, live, shop, see your elders, and care for the young all in the same place. I've heard of more and more of these communities.

❏ *Offer employee-alumni hospice.* Offer a company-subsidized hospice for employee alumni with a certain number of years of service.

❏ *Offer early hospice in-home support.* Create an opportunity for company-sponsored in-home support for early hospice needs of employees and employee-alumni.

Total Rewards Related to Multiple Household Types

❏ *Provide flexible, results-based promotion opportunities.* Companies can create a promotion schedule that allows someone with unusual or part-time hours to still be promoted. The concern of every parent, particularly a single parent, is how hours and flexible extra time-off will affect the opportunity for career advancement. Base the promotions on results, not hours worked.

❑ *Allow employees to define family memberships.* Employees can determine those they would like to receive medical coverage under the company plan. Work with carriers to make these changes.

❑ *Make optional life insurance available for selected household members.* Companies can allow employees to purchase optional life insurance for those whom they designate as members of their household.

❑ *Expand long-term disability coverage.* Provide for long-term disability insurance that covers employees who work variable hours and flexible schedules.

❑ *Redefine spousal benefit for retirement.* Allow employees to determine the beneficiary of their retirement payments, similarly to the way life insurance works, where employees choose their beneficiary.

❑ *Broaden definition of bringing a youngster to work.* Maybe companies can allow employees to bring more than just children to work, perhaps a sibling, spouse, partner, or even parent, who wants to find out more about their family member's job, company, or career. Maybe the definition can be broadened to include children who are from less fortunate situations that are provided the opportunity to see a professional setting.

Getting Employee Input on Total-Rewards Priorities

Invite about twenty employees with unique household situations to a focus group discussion of issues around benefits, compensation, and total rewards. Ask them to come up with fiscally responsible ideas that would help them.

Questions posed could include:

1. What benefits restrict your ability to cover your family?

2. If the company could provide any service, what would you ask for?

3. If you were in charge, which of our current benefits and compensation offerings would you keep? Which would you get rid of? Which would you change?

Particularly insightful in this type of focus group is a ranking exercise. Provide a list of total-rewards options or use the options in question 3 above. Then ask the members of the focus group to rank what's most important. Emphasize the unusual in the list. For example, include:

❑ Sick child help

❑ Homework hotline

❑ Driver service

Also include traditional benefits such as medical, life, disability, retirement, and time off. By ranking benefits in this manner, you are in better position to try new benefits where they are needed the most.

TOTAL REWARDS RELATED TO GENERATIONS

❑ *Offer life-stage-based benefits.* Make choices available to employees based on where they are in their life situation. Include options for pay, benefits, work schedule, training, time off/vacation. Figure 8-3 provides a grid of the types of rewards that may be priorities to the various age brackets.

TOTAL REWARDS RELATED TO DIVERSITY

❑ *Publish pay ranges.* Just as colleges and universities publish student diversity demographics, companies can publish pay ranges by constituency, such as men, women, minorities, and disabled employees. These published figures can be by category of job, and then by employee constituency within that job category. Share and brag about great results.

❑ *Redesign job descriptions.* Companies can revise job descriptions with a sensitive eye to be sure they are allowing for diverse categories of candidates to apply. Redo current job descriptions to ensure that educational or job experience requirements are truly necessary.

For example, at CGI we have a job titled "Consultant." The long-standing job description for a "Consultant" requires five-to-eight years of experience and at least a college degree. In looking at our current staff, however, we have two extremely successful

Figure 8-3. Generations and potential total-rewards priorities.

20-Somethings	Training
	Promotion/career coaching
	Auto insurance
	Lease review
	Extra work hours
	Extra vacation
	Gym
	Social lives tied more to work—plan functions, happy hours
	Continuing education
30-Somethings	Mortgage assistance
	Career planning
	Infertility/adoption assistance
	Savings plans education and options
	Extra work hours
	Vacation/gym facilities
40-Somethings	Housecleaning
	Interior decorating help
	Elder/child care
	Time flexibility
	Schedule flexibility
	Retirement benefits
	Savings plan
50-Somethings	College tuition assistance/subsidies
	Retirement planning
	Financial planning
	Investment counseling
	Time flexibility
	Significant time off
	Travel planning
	Life insurance priorities
	Extra disability

(continued)

Figure 8-3. (Continued).

60- to 70-Somethings	Social interaction sponsored by work
	Flexible hours
	Retirement planning
	Less life insurance
	Less disability
80 + -Somethings	Reverse life insurance
	Extra major medical insurance
	Living assistance
	Reverse mortgage
	Driver/shuttle service
	Flexible hours, part-time work

consultants who fall outside this out-dated job description . Neither consultant has a college degree. At the same time, they each have more than eight years of experience. They are from diverse backgrounds and excel in meeting their goals. We obviously need to re-evaluate our longstanding job requirements.

Total Rewards Related to Trust and Respect

❑ *Communicate.* Divulge company information on salaries, promotion requirements, who gets them, and announce increases. The more openly a company shares details about the "mysterious" pay and benefits plans, the less likely it is to have abuse of the system. Instead of guarding pay schedules, publish them. Let employees know you have a fair and equitable pay system.

❑ *Provide company-sponsored vacation houses.* Companies can rent homes in various vacation destinations and provide these homes for employees on a weekly basis as an affordable getaway. The Rouse Company, a shopping center and real estate developer based in Columbia, Maryland, hosted such a program for years, dubbing them "Rouse Houses."

❑ *Create mentor program with rewards built in.* Companies could recognize the success of the mentoring relationship by including rewards for both sides of the relationship. For example, picture a Nexter coaching a Senior how to use a new software package. As a result, the Senior can process twice the work. Why not give each employee a half day off with pay? Another example: When a mentored employee gets promoted, give the mentor a reward as well.

OFFER A MENU OF TOTAL REWARD CHOICES

From standard to custom, give each employee parameters for their total-rewards package and allow them to structure it from there. Include base pay, bonus pay, work schedule as well as a menu of options that can be "bought" depending on their particular needs, priorities, or situation.

This menu could include:

❏ Pet insurance

❏ Tuition reimbursement

❏ Scholarships for employees' children

❏ Identity theft insurance

❏ In-home security system

❏ Wellness choices: exams, health clubs

❏ Eye glasses, hearing aids

❏ Child and elder care

❏ Car, car insurance, maintenance

❏ Computer classes, support for home computer problems

❏ Coverage for elective surgery

❏ Coverage for cosmetic plastic surgery

❏ Coverage for experimental treatment, surgery, drugs

CONCLUSION

Employee benefits and compensation in the future will take us into uncharted territory. The needs and demands of the future workforce will give rise to an emphasis on total rewards and packages tailored to individual needs. For example, younger workers may prefer auto insurance coverage above all else, particularly life insurance. Benefits might also come to include paying for genetic counseling, nutritional food, and spiritual guidance for employees to whom these issues are important.

Total rewards will tie compensation and benefits in ways that it has not before. We will retain workers with means other than salary. The goal of pay and benefits will change from one of merely compensating to one of rewarding and motivating. A company's approach to total rewards will lie in a strong guiding strategy. In determining strategy, companies will include their employee concerns and needs in addition to company productivity and profitability goals. This will be both a challenge and an exciting opportunity.

NOTES

1. "No Prizes for Runners Up," *The Economist,* February 2002, p. 57.
2. Ted Buyniski, Interview, August 2003.
3. Ibid.
4. City of Hope, Cancer Screening and Prevention Program, "Hereditary Breast Caner in Ashkenazi-Jewish Persons," *www.infosci.coh.org/ccgp/cspp/akinfo.asp.*
5. Leonard Wierner, "Pining Away for Pensions," *U.S. News and World Report*, December 24, 2001, p. 34.
6. Jon Hilsenrath, "Economics Professor's Retirement Project Puts Future Pay Raises into Savings Plan, *The Wall Street Journal*, January 11, 2002, p. A2.
7. "Pension Pettiness," *The Wall Street Journal*, February 5, 2002, p. A1.

CHAPTER 9

THE IMPACT ON
LEARNING AND TRAINING

My partner, Alex, is a visual learner. He can't function without a pen in his hand or a whiteboard in his conference room. He has to write things down, illustrate, and convey information in writing. In order to tell me how to find a client's location, he needs to draw a map. I, on the other hand, am an auditory learner. I retain what I hear. In order for me to find the client's location, I need someone to tell me, "Turn left on Elm at the big church; go three miles; turn right on Maple at the convenience store; it's the third building on the left." Other people need the combination of visual and auditory components to learn. By whatever means it's delivered, employee learning and training will be a key company priority of the future.

Corporate training has long been a source of frustration. People learn at different rates; some forget what they have learned. Those being trained are out of the office and others need to pick up the slack or wait until the trainee returns. There are always employees who leave after the company has invested in their training. Even the best programs seem to only move you forward an inch, instead of the foot forward you had hoped. Plus, training and development are expensive. All of these factors have led many to the common organizational view that training is a necessary evil that should be kept to a minimum.

Training, however, is much more than a necessary evil. Done correctly, it expands the skill level of your employees, therefore making them more valuable overall to your company. It is a ticket to employee loyalty and retention. It can be a recruiting advantage. Furthermore, it can take a company a long way toward the culture of respect and responsibility that the future workforce will demand.

If training is to be relevant, effective, and efficient, employers will need to gear training to the variety of ways in which people learn. This is another case of one size doesn't fit all—a common theme throughout this book, as you've no doubt noticed.

A Look Back

For years, many corporations had wonderful training and development programs. These programs included a wide variety of courses, such as management and supervisory training, job-specific skill training, and on-the-job training. Workers flew to exotic locations to attend conferences and seminars. Tuition reimbursement was available for continuing education.

Then came the shortsighted, bottom-line oriented 1990s. Tightening budgets, "right-sizing," and profit priorities led to the cancellation of many training programs. As company loyalty and employee loyalty spun downward and almost out of sight, companies became increasingly less willing to invest in all but the most job-specific training. Career and professional development were more often viewed as an expense that would benefit a competitor when the employee left, rather than as an investment in human capital, loyalty, and long-term company success.

The new workforce, however, will demand resurgence in training, and advancing technology will pave the way. As employers seek to attract the best and brightest talent, education and training will be valuable assets in recruitment efforts. Further, companies that embrace training and development as priorities will retain their best workers as well.

A Few Definitions

As we delve into the topic of training, it will be helpful to put some definition and parameters around three terms that are often used interchangeably: education, learning, and training.

Education is the broadest of terms. Education includes elementary, middle, and high school, as well as college and advanced degrees. Education prepares us for life as well as for success in any number of careers. Education is the foundation that teaches us the basics of reading, writing, and arithmetic, and then hopefully goes on to teach us how to think.

Training, at the other end of the spectrum, is much more specific than education. Training teaches a specific skill that will help an individual develop proficiency in a certain job or job category.

Learning can include both broader education and more specific training. Generally, though, I think of learning as somewhere in between. Learning most often teaches employees a skill that will travel through life as well as employment.

EDUCATION: A FOUNDATION IN FLUX

Changes in basic education necessary to fix a system in peril are being debated in all areas of our society. These changes will affect the future workforce as well as day-to-day operations of companies—especially those companies that are strategic and forward thinking.

Changes in education over the next several years will be driven by several factors:

1. *Decentralization and Educational Options.* The variety of educational choices will continue to increase dramatically. As of April 2003, 850,000 students were in home schools and 580,000 were in charter schools. Irving Buchen, senior research associate at EdVisions Cooperative, feels that by 2025 education will be completely decentralized and present a huge number of choices to students, parents, and all citizens in general.

2. *Changes in Leadership and Leadership Roles.* There will be a shortage of 40,000 principals by 2005. Schools are hiring MBAs rather than MAs in education. In some instances, titles are being changed from superintendent to CEO. Following the idea of distributed leadership, teacher-leaders and learning teams will be responsible for school operations.

3. *Change in Teacher's Role.* Teachers will become leaders and even owners in the education process. Some teachers will actually start schools and run them as profit making, entrepreneurial ventures. An entrepreneurial spirit where the students come out ahead will

replace traditional teacher roles of subjugated employee and union member. Teacher professional partnerships are beginning to form that offer specialized services and programs, which are run within a school, across several schools, and even outside of schools.

4. *Reconfiguration in Learning Spaces, Places, and Times.* Student-driven schools will grow. Team learning will gain prominence. Technology will facilitate immediacy, instant feedback, customized curriculum, and reduced class size to as small as one student.

The Future Role of Companies in Education

As companies become hungry for workers, innovative ideas will get them involved with education at the most fundamental level.

❑ *Fostering Interest in Specific Fields.* For example, concern continues to grow that American schools are not graduating enough skilled scientists and engineers—a finding reinforced by economist Paul M. Rohmer in a Stanford University study cited in *Business Week,* November 13, 2000. Overcoming this lack of skilled workers will increasingly become the responsibility of companies themselves. Company sponsorships, internships, and school-based programs will play a critical role in education that guides graduates toward skills and careers that these companies require.

ATOFINA Chemical's Science Teacher Program

One such program is the Science Teacher Program of ATOFINA Chemical. It focuses on teacher training and development, which in turn benefits students in the long term.

ATOFINA introduced the program in 1996 to address science illiteracy. Teachers can both continue their professional development and learn methods for presenting science in an exciting and real-life context through custom-created science kits.

"These teachers and ATOFINA scientists have a rare opportunity to work together exploring the mysteries of nature and science," says Jane Crawford, director of corporate communications for ATOFINA Chemical and director of the company's Science Teacher Program. "Teachers will leave ATOFINA's program equipped with hands-on science kits and activities to enhance science instruction back in the classroom, which in turn benefits students for many years."[1]

❏ *Corporate-Sponsored Urban High Schools.* Natalie Allen, president of the Philadelphia Academies, believes that within the next ten years the think-tank ideas about reforming urban schools will be exhausted, but that the dire problems will remain unsolved. As a result, she foresees a dramatic change: Corporations will take charge of basic education because the need for educated talent will be so extreme.

In her vision, corporations will be funded by tax dollars as well as their own dollars in this educational venture. They will take the experience they have in developing and delivering skill-based training and translate it to general education—targeting students from as early as eighth grade all the way through high school. Smaller corporations will form education consortiums or pair with a larger corporation. In this way, she believes the basic skills of reading, writing, and arithmetic will enjoy renewed emphasis and in fact might provide an entirely new generation of Americans that are educated properly.

Whether through corporate education of the youth, home schooling, private schooling, or urban and suburban schooling, Allen believes that if we can get our youth educated appropriately in core values at an early age, we can improve everything from basic education to dressing, conflict resolution, working in a team, speaking properly, and being prepared for the workplace. With so much money at stake and development needs so strong in our organizations, Allen's ideas pose a unique opportunity for companies to thrive.[2]

Corporate Involvement in Education: A Success Story
I found a wonderful example of the possibilities that accompany corporate involvement in education. The Candle Corp, a software company in El Segundo, California, knew that 10 percent of its

employees were teenagers—many from Los Angeles' poorest neighborhoods. Aubrey Chernick, Candle's founder and CEO, also knew he had an impending severe labor shortage. Meanwhile, Howard Lapin, principal of South Central's James A. Foschay Learning Center, had transformed his school from one of LA's worst to one of its best pathways to college. Armed with that turnaround, he sought actual business experience for his students. In 1996, he connected with Chernick, and Candle began offering paid internships.

The success has been phenomenal. Chosen by merit, the interns stay until they graduate, although many stayed on through college and doubled their salary. Four have come to work for Candle full-time. Starting with 15 students in 1997, Candle had 68 interns in the program in 2000. In part thanks to Candle's Teen Apprentice Program, Foschay's entire Class of 2000, 150 strong, got into college, more than half into four-year schools.

❑ *Tuition Reimbursement.* The concept is not new, but the flexibility and availability will be. Companies can not only offer tuition reimbursement, but broaden it as well. Revised tuition reimbursement programs will include not only degree programs, but also nondegree programs, select audited courses, and pass/fail courses.

❑ *Bringing College to the Workforce.* High Concrete Structures, Inc., a leading manufacturer of precast concrete products in Denver, Pennsylvania, brought a university into the workplace. By making arrangements with Albright College, the High employees who register and are accepted, get a college degree at work. To make matters even better, a High employee, the director of production, is also an Albright marketing professor in the evenings. He negotiated to have the program run at the High plant.

❑ *Bonus for Learning.* Encouragement of ongoing education, training, and learning. The heart of this type of program is a tuition-reimbursement system that not only pays for school, but also gives time off to employees pursuing degrees or professional development programs. Upon completing a degree, an employee receives a significant one-time bonus.

A University of Southern California Marshall School of Business study reported that this type of tuition program helps the company recruit top candidates, who see it as a significant reason for joining the company.

At one leading technology firm, over one-third of the salaried workforce participates in the tuition-reimbursement program, and nearly 10 percent of the employees have earned a degree through the program. Those who received a degree have had higher performance ratings, earned greater merit pay increases, and advanced more rapidly than other employees.

The tuition reimbursement program is also a significant retention tool. The turnover rate for those participating in the program was only 8 percent, compared to 13 percent for those not involved. Since a part-time graduate degree course typically takes at least four years to complete, this has been a significant benefit in retaining the high-potential workers who are most likely to pursue degrees.

What happens after training and/or degrees are completed? Do these newly skilled and educated, and therefore very expensive, employees jump ship? It depends on what the company does with them. The Marshall Study on training and development found that employees were much more likely to stay with the employer who paid for their training and education if the training and education were used and rewarded. Upon completing a degree under the tuition reimbursement plan, less than 4 percent left the company if they were promoted or given a significant raise. Of those who received neither a raise nor promotion, 20 percent left the company.

❑ *Employee Library and Resource Center.* Companies can facilitate worker education through the development of an employee library. Books, magazines, how-to manuals, and software tutorials can address a variety of business issues and be available for workers to check out.

THE FUTURE ROLE OF COMPANIES IN LEARNING

One step closer to education and broader than job-specific training, learning is a growing priority for companies. While not so extreme and forward thinking as funding and running general youth education, learning is a valuable way for companies to get ahead of the curve relative to the emerging workforce. The combination of the labor shortage and the increasing demand for an involved culture that values and respects its employees leads to learning as a critical component for corporate development in both the short- and long-term.

Learning and Personal Fulfillment

As we are going to be living for such a long time, people will begin to think in terms of multiple careers. Across genders and generations, the emerging workforce will be seeking job enhancement and career development. At the same time, personal satisfaction and meaningful work will be the ultimate priority. Robert Schoonmaker, my husband, has worked with literally hundreds of individuals in career development as well as what he calls "life planning." He sees a consistent series of stages where employees go from working hard toward a certain goal, to attaining it, and to then stepping back and asking, "Is that it?" Healthy longevity, in his view, provides the ultimate opportunity for one to pursue a life-long dream or follow a calling.

Robert finds that a learning approach in which people build on their strengths is a very effective start in this pursuit. Focusing on what one does well takes an individual's strengths and matches job skills to those strengths. It works on the premise that people will excel in pursuits they feel good about, and will feel good about pursuits where they excel.

❑ *Admiral School.* At CGI we have a special program we call "Admiral School." The program is open to all employees, but they must apply to be included. Once accepted, the "students" report directly to Alex, our chairman, for their learning, which is scheduled after work hours. The curriculum includes homework and tests. Subjects include client interaction skills, technical skills, complex benefits knowledge—in short, topics that are Alex's strengths. It is also an opportunity to be with the boss, who is a charismatic, remarkable person. Admiral School is very popular. There is always a waiting list to get in.

❏ *Corporate Universities.* Corporate universities give companies the ability to customize content to match the needs of the business and individual worker. Some courses are developed and delivered as internal programs. Others involve a partnership with a higher education institution.

Corporate universities award course credit to participants in recognition of the knowledge acquired. As more and more companies develop and expand corporate universities, they are not only moving much of the content online, but also investing in more face-to-face courses.

Internal programs often tap the expertise of various employees as teachers for courses. For example:

❏ Someone from accounting teaches math skills or offers instruction in completing forms and reports.

❏ Someone from IT offers technology updates about what's new and what's coming, or guides "how-to" sessions for current software applications.

❏ Various department heads offer "101" seminars, offering a basic overview of their discipline and its role within the company.

Here are some other course ideas, which could be included as part of a formal corporate university arrangement or simply presented as stand-alone learning opportunities:

❏ *Basic Writing Skills.* One area where I see a consistent lack of skill is in basic writing. Companies might have someone on staff who is capable of teaching such a course through the corporate university. Outside seminars and courses are available as well. However it is accomplished, teaching employees how to express themselves in clear and concise sentences can have far-reaching benefits, from avoiding communication breakdowns to keeping customers well serviced and satisfied.

❏ *Presentation Skills.* I place this right up there with basic writing. Most employees, at all levels, can benefit from learning and practicing presentation skills.

❏ *Customer Service.* Through examples, shared stories, and role-playing, companies can guide employees in going the extra mile for customer service. If I were sharing such a story, I'd relate my recent experience with an equipment rental shop. While on a trip to Florida, we rented a power washer to clean our house. Once we got it home and all set up, we found it was broken—it simply wouldn't work. We called and the store agreed to send someone to check out the problem. When he arrived, the repairman found that he could not fix the machine we had rented. Not to worry. Just to be safe, he had brought another machine—a much larger one. He carried it in and set it up for us. Then, realizing that the unit was too big to fit in our trunk and recognizing our inconvenience with the initial broken machine, he offered to return in the morning to pick up the bigger machine. No charge. That's what I call going the extra mile. What could have been a customer service nightmare became a wonderful experience. We called his boss the next day to acknowledge the repairman's excellent service. The boss initially thought we were calling to complain—he later stated that complaint calls were the norm for him.

Employees at all levels can benefit from this kind of learning. In order to keep up momentum after training, I would encourage companies to follow up with rewards for employees who "go the extra mile."

❑ *Blasting Stereotypes.* Similar to the fad of sensitivity training of the 1980s, employees need to learn ways of overcoming biases and ways of thinking outside of stereotypes. These include all kinds of notions from "old-timers won't or can't learn technology" to "a handicapped person can't manage a group of employees." Outside facilitators are recommended to lead diverse groups of employees in discussions that build bridges and break down barriers.

❑ *Business Skills.* A whole host of opportunities exist for potential business skill courses. These could include:
  ❑ How to read financial reports
  ❑ Understanding stocks and bonds
  ❑ Shareholder requirements
  ❑ Understanding profit and loss
  ❑ Reading and preparing a budget

- ❏ Making investment choices
- ❏ How to get the most from your benefits
- ❏ Understanding company policies

❏ *Life Skills.* There are also many, many potential seminar/course topics relating to life skills for employees. A few examples include:
- ❏ How to save for your future
- ❏ Caregiver training
- ❏ Time management
- ❏ Organization management
- ❏ Conflict resolution
- ❏ Nutrition
- ❏ Enhancing your own longevity
- ❏ Reducing stress
- ❏ CPR and defibrillator training
- ❏ Identity theft protection

❏ *Training the Trainers.* To the extent possible, I recommend using as many insider trainers as possible, leveraging and recognizing employee strengths and allowing them to share and teach those strengths to others. As such, an effective train-the-trainer curriculum will be important.

Ways to Enhance Employee Learning Programs

There are many things companies can do to improve the overall learning experience of their employees. Here are a few of the best:

❏ *Mentors.* Mentor programs offer another valuable means of corporate learning. Once a staple in the business world, mentoring suffered a slump in the wake of budget cuts, job jumping, and layoffs. With the emerging workforce, however, mentoring will enjoy resurgence for several reasons:
- ❏ Mentors enhance employee loyalty.
- ❏ Mentors share valuable insight and experiences, as well as teach skills.
- ❏ Mentors increase workers' feelings of respect and individual attention.

❏ More mentors with valuable information to share will be available because of longevity and postponed retirement.

❏ Mentors allow companies to hold on to and pass along the wisdom of its valued older workers.

Mentors and Ethics

A 2003 Harvard University study surveyed 100 young professionals to determine not only their goals and aspirations for overcoming obstacles, but also their choice of values. While they were fully aware of right and wrong, those in the study admitted a readiness to compromise their values both ethically and professionally in order to get ahead. Then, they expressed a full intention to follow a strict code of values once in a position of power and authority. Dr. Howard Gardner, who led the study, believes this willingness to cheat to achieve has come about because the adults in the lives of these youth, including teachers and mentors, never worked with them to build and internalize a strong moral compass. Young professionals place priority on money and fame at levels not previously possible. Gardner also says that traditional ethical guides, such as religious, family, and community values, have become less influential since the 1980s.

"Mentoring," says Gardner, "is disappearing, a casualty of the faster-paced more transient workplace in some areas."[3] I believe, however, that we will begin to see mentoring grow with the new workforce. Employees and managers alike are recognizing the wisdom of moral and ethical guidance as well as the skill and experience sharing that comes with strong mentoring.

❏ *"Mentoring Up."* The rising and racing advances in technology have ushered in another type of mentoring that is growing in usefulness and popularity. "Mentoring up" refers to assigning a younger, technologically savvy professional to serve as mentor/trainer to an older, experienced, but technologically challenged coworker. Companies are taking this concept beyond technology. *Reverse mentoring*, as it is often called (I prefer the term "mutual mentoring"), is also being used as a means of keeping senior-level and senior-aged workers up to speed on what's "hip." Companies from General Electric and Chase Manhattan Bank, to Best Buy and the Wharton School at the University of Pennsylvania are finding reverse mentoring rewarding on many levels. First of all, because both employees share their own knowledge, experience, and skill sets, both benefit. Company loyalty is enhanced through the interpersonal relationships. Knowledge is shared not only up-down and down-up, but also side-to-side across departments and disciplines of an organization. This bolsters creative thinking and fosters a culture of respect and sharing.

❑ *Study Groups.* Similarly to the process commonly used by students in law school, companies can create "study groups" of employees mixed by diversity, generation, background, etc. They can then assign them an issue related to training or another areas of work, give them time to work together to study their assigned issue, and make recommendations to management.

❑ *Book Clubs.* Companies can organize employee book clubs to discuss business as well and pleasure books. Mixing up the representation in the group will enhance diversity understanding.

❑ *One-on-One Career Coaching.* Companies can make a career coach available to individual employees for learning at a more intimate level. At these sessions, employees could discuss results of aptitude tests, what they are best at, and what they enjoy. With the guidance of the coach they could map out a potential career path, and list the steps necessary to follow it.

❑ *Retreats.* I have found that employees do their best learning by going offsite, out of the office. While classrooms, conference rooms, and computer modules all have their place, I encourage offsite retreats whenever possible, even if held in the home of a manager or employee.

Make Orientation a Better Learning Experience

Orientation, the one-day company overview for new hires, has traditionally focused on signing up for benefits, reviewing the major policies, and showing people around. Here are some ideas for improving the experience:

❑ *More Than One Day.* Companies should make orientation much more comprehensive, and allow it to take place over more than one day. Perhaps orientation can include a series of breakfast or lunch meetings that take place over a week or two. The employee is then more settled, less nervous, and more ready to listen.

❑ *Expanded Subject Areas.* In addition to the "normal stuff," company orientation provides the perfect opportunity to stress company values, explain the company mission and vision, gather objective feedback on company perspective and reputation, as well as discuss career development, benefits, and training opportunities.

❑ *Annual Update.* Further, companies should consider an annual orientation update for all employees to review and share what's new.

USE TESTING TO MEASURE ONGOING LEARNING

Testing is most often part of the hiring and recruiting process. However, once the person is on board, a broader use of testing could provide tremendous insight to both the employee and management, and enhance learning as well.

❑ *Test for results instead of skills.* To help place all employees on objective and equal footing regardless of their work schedule or background, companies can test for results at the end of projects, fiscal years, or employment anniversaries. This will help guide raise and promotion considerations.

❑ *Test for promotions.* Provide employees with the opportunity to volunteer for testing when they feel that they are ready for promotion. This could help objectify the process.

❑ *Test for aptitudes instead of prior experience/education.* By testing for aptitudes, companies can uncover areas of employee strength and promise that reveal potential in other areas or departments. Since people are generally more satisfied when they are doing something they are good at and enjoy, employees win when they learn about and pursue their aptitudes. Companies win, too, since employees performing up to their potential and aptitudes will tend to be both

more productive and more loyal. Don't forget about Rudy back in
Chapter 7!

Want More Ideas? Ask Your Employees!

Employee focus groups can be a wonderful way to not only come
up with ideas for topics, but to locate hidden teaching talents and
focus on employee needs and wants for training. To create an employee focus group on Learning, gather a group of employee volunteers from several different demographics and job levels. Again,
include no more than twenty people in one discussion group.

Conversation starters for the group can include:

1. At what time of day do you do your best learning?

2. Where do you do your best learning? In a comfortable
   chair, in a quiet conference room, at your computer?

3. How do you best learn? When you read, hear, view, interact?

4. What suggestions do you have for subjects/topics for company-sponsored learning: work, personal, skill-based, con-
   ceptual?

THE FUTURE ROLE OF COMPANIES IN TRAINING

While embracing the importance of learning, companies should also recognize training as a critical component of employee productivity and company
profitability. Training today comes in many forms—and training in the future
is likely to be even more diverse. The smart companies are moving already
to study and test out a wide variety of training delivery methods. As these
delivery methods are improved and new ones are developed, these companies are in the forefront of training today's workers and are ready to train
the workforce of tomorrow.

TECHNOLOGY AND TRAINING

In order to make training as consistent and efficient as possible, companies
are leveraging new technology and systems.

❏ *E-Learning.* Online learning is its own booming business, and with good reason. Employees can work at their own pace, review whenever they want, get instant feedback, and complete the course work without leaving the office or home. E-learning also gives employees the ultimate flexibility as to when they complete the training—they can wait until they truly need a specific skill before they learn it. The training doesn't disappear before it gets used.

One young professional I know spent two days out of the office at Excel software training. She had no immediate use for the program, which is most helpful with spreadsheets and budgets. Several months later, when she had to create a project budget, she had completely forgotten how Excel worked.

CISCO: A Technology Training Story

Here's a good example of the usefulness of technology in training. Tom Kelly, vice president of World Wide Training for CISCO Systems, a leader in Internet networking, was hired in 1997 to tune up CISCO's training. Four thousand internal salespeople, 15,000 partner organizations, and thousands of customers needed training on products, technology, and Internet-based business practices. At the time he was hired, 85 percent of the training at CISCO was classroom-based. Kelly's group saw e-learning as a major solution to its training challenges. In order to make the training more effective and efficient, sales reps take competency tests to see what and how much training they need. From there, training is customized for each individual. They also began a system of "emergency learning" where a twenty-minute session of key information can be delivered just before a crucial meeting.

In order to streamline the process of determining what CISCO already knew and where that knowledge was in the company, Field E-LearningConnection (FELC) was started. FELC is a Web site of information sorted by audience and organized into maps by job title, work area, specific technology, and product. Every piece of content is tagged with a digital short hand, allowing for instant reuse or redeployment.[4]

❑ *Computer Simulations.* Pratt & Whitney is an example of a company that is creating computer simulation to teach means of decision making involved in developing new aircraft engines. With simulation, hands-on instruction of new tools enhances effectiveness. In addition, employees from different departments can take part in the training, appreciate their own role in a wider business context, and appreciate different perspectives, including the customer's.

TRAINING, LEARNING, AND RETENTION

A University of Southern California Marshall School of Business study found the following characteristics in successful company-supported learning:

❑ Strong mentoring relationships

❑ Challenging work assignments

❑ Managers who provide the time and encouragement for individuals to develop their skills

When all this is part of company-supported learning, it is a strong predictor of employee commitment and business effectiveness.[5]

One of the most common reasons a person leaves an organization is a real or perceived lack of career advancement opportunity. As companies become less bureaucratic and more flat in structure, and as teams and projects become mainstays to productivity, learning and training across several disciplines of the company become invaluable. If traditional promotions of "moving up the food chain" are less available, career opportunities can be greatly enhanced if learning and training for broadened or even "new" careers within the company are made possible and encouraged.

Companies such as Hewlett Packard and Lockheed Martin are posting jobs across their organizations and encouraging managers to help their employees to apply to other departments. AT&T is creating detailed databases so they can match current employees to job openings and projects. The databases are updated to include any training employees have had and any new skills they have learned.

LEARNING AND TRAINING AND THE FIVE TRENDS

As you adapt your learning and training to the new workforce, you'll have to be aware of the individual needs and capabilities of your employees. Here again, flexibility will be the key in choosing and delivering company training.

LEARNING RELATED TO LONGEVITY

As more and more older employees are included in your new workforce, they will become an integral part of your training and learning sessions. Here are a few ideas on making this experience better all around:

- ❏ *Adapt learning materials.* We learn differently as we age. Print needs to be bigger. Volume may need to be louder. These kinds of accommodations will not only ensure correct learning and training, it will also bolster individual sense of value and respect.

- ❏ *Put aside "old" stereotypes.* There is no evidence that older people learn more slowly or that they aren't willing to learn new things. In fact, record numbers of older Americans are taking courses in all areas from computers to self-improvement to university courses.

- ❏ *Offer transition training.* Transition training helps older employees transition to new positions and roles within the company. We often discard the older worker, and fail to focus on transition training to continue to harvest the counsel and wisdom of retirees of the company. We do a poor job of listening to that wisdom. New people often want to do it on their own without seeking the input and advice of those who have gone before.

  Even the top brass often can use some transition training. As CEOs or other executives step down, they may stay on as consultants and may need help transitioning to a role where they don't call the shots.

- ❏ *Offer frequent breaks during formal training/coursework.* Older employees may need a little downtime scheduled throughout the day. They can then return to their training, refreshed and ready to learn.

- ❏ *Serve healthy food during training.* The trend has been toward cutting back on refreshments served during training. It's time to bring it back. However, instead of doughnuts, cookies, and pastries, try serving healthy snacks, such as a variety of fruits.

LEARNING RELATED TO MULTIPLE HOUSEHOLD TYPES

The diverse makeup of your employees' households may affect both their availability for training and also what kind of training they will require.

- ❑ *Make where and when flexible.* If employees need to pursue e-training at home and that home environment is complex, it may not be effective. Other options will need to be made available, whether at the office, offsite, or in a conference room. This acknowledges that individual employees have different home situations, time constraints, and support systems.

- ❑ *Offer parenting skills, caregiver skills.* Employees who are faced with difficult home situations or with situations they are not adequately prepared to handle can often use training in areas such as parenting and caregiving. This helps your employees by providing valuable and needed training they may not have access to anywhere else. And any training that enables your people to better handle their home situations makes them more productive and probably more loyal employees.

  Here are a few other ways you can make training and learning easier for employees with complicated home situations:
  - ❑ Offer baby sitting or elder care during training.
  - ❑ Allow family members to attend and learn.
  - ❑ Offer translators/translations.

LEARNING RELATED TO GENERATIONS

In addition to working side by side in the workplace of the future (if they aren't doing so already), the different generations will be learning together. Here are some ideas for getting the most out of this cross-generational training:

- ❑ *Accommodate different learning styles.* The ability to customize training, even on the same topic, for members of different generations will be an important factor in determining which companies succeed in the future and which companies become sought-after employers.

❏ *Set up mutual mentoring.* Companies can set up formal mentoring relationships across generations that benefit both partners in the arrangement.

❏ *Create bridge buddies.* Companies can open communication and enhance understanding across multiple generations by creating "bridge buddies." While it could involve actually learning to play bridge, the concept is more about building bridges by encouraging social relationships between employees of different generations. Partners or multigenerational "families" can be assigned or employee-chosen. Companies can offer bridge buddies common times for lunch, discounted tickets, speakers, or shared break time.

❏ *Offer a course on company protocol.* Members of the Silent Generation would probably never say no to a lunch invitation from the CEO, but the younger generation often does. I am hearing routinely from clients about the CEO asking someone to a social event or a lunch and getting a resounding "no." Regardless of how extensive someone's education may have been, there are certain things that they may never have been taught. A course on protocol can cover topics like this. In addition, employees need to learn how to mix, mingle, introduce, network, and make conversation.

LEARNING RELATED TO DIVERSITY

"Diversity training" is not a new concept to corporate America. Many companies have been holding such sessions for years. Some succeed; others fail. The goal, however, remains: increasing awareness and understanding to make us comfortable with one another and our differences. In this way, we will not only enhance the work experience for individual employees, but also provide for diverse teams and task forces working together for maximum creativity, effectiveness, and range of thinking.

❏ *English as a Second Language (ESL).* As mentioned in Chapter 8, offering ESL to employees for whom English is not the primary language can be a part of an employee's total rewards package.

Communicating Effectively with Different Groups, Genders, or Cultures

For example, men and women are known to listen differently and question differently. Thus, communication breakdown is inevitable. Men tend to interrupt, while women are more hesitant and are better listeners. Molly D. Shepard, at The Leaders Edge, offers leadership development training to senior level women to help them understand these differences and acquire skills and tools to bridge the communication gap. Shepard takes small groups of women into a retreat setting and, with the help of simulations, enhances their presentation styles, communication, and negotiation skills. During the training, she hires men to act in a variety of pre-set roles, for example, the autocrat, the interrupter, or the nonlistener. Then she teaches the women how to respond effectively to those men and reach mutual understanding.

❑ *Use video as a training tool.* Shepard videotapes the women's style variances in reacting to the various typecast males. The women view both pre- and post-training behavior. It is a powerful visual tool for encouraging behavior change and increased sensitivity to differences.

❑ *Offer employee sensitivity training.* Companies can develop a group of employee teachers from diverse backgrounds to teach sensitivity and communication training for their own group. These employees can train others in their demographic group about assimilation, and teach others from different demographic groups about sensitivities of and communication within their special demographic.

❑ *Diversify mentor match-ups.* Leverage diversity of organization to mix it up better than in the past. When assigning mentors, match by personality types or aptitudes instead of cultural or demographic similarity. In fact, specifically look for diversity in the pairings.

❑ *Teach sensitivity to differences.* Awareness of cultural differences, style difference, and even language will take us far beyond the simple personality profiles so common to supervisory and management training of the past. Understanding breeds acceptance and respect.

❑ *Teach cross-cultural communications.* Recognizing the implications of certain phrases, actions, and dress to those who are different from us will build a sensitive and harmonious work culture. How to hand a business card to someone from Japan, the significance of different religious customs, appropriate touching for the workplace, and keeping inappropriate humor at bay are all examples of the types of learning necessary to create a culture of acceptance.

LEARNING RELATED TO TRUST, RESPECT, AND ETHICS

Since learning itself is based on trust, respect, and ethics, the final trend—a growing sense of higher purpose in the workplace—touches upon all aspects of learning and training. Companies should keep this synergy in mind when developing programs for the future.

- ❏ *Expand manager and supervisor skills training.* Reinforcing the company's core values and ethics is an important part of management and supervisory training. Role-playing ethical case questions will allow managers and supervisors to learn and integrate the company's value system.

- ❏ *Teach the merits of constant feedback.* Annual reviews may have their place, but a system that provides input to help encourage employee growth only once a year (if that!) is archaic. Management and supervisory training needs to include a system for providing ongoing feedback to employees.

- ❏ *Avoid rigid job guidelines.* June Barry, senior vice president at Citizens Bank, says "adult psychology, knowing the business, and appropriate coaching skills are the future for human resources. This is the opposite of the old-fashioned personnel department or HR department that relied on understanding the laws and demanding that people comply, enforcing a rigid job description, and insisting that we do performance appraisals according to a certain format."[6]

- ❏ *Include information on all five trends.* Information on the workforce at large and the changes affecting it will be an important part of enhancing management understanding, sensitivity, and ability to communicate effectively with the emerging workforce.

- ❏ *Give positive feedback.* Not only management can benefit from this kind of training. Appreciative feedback that becomes part of the culture can greatly enhance productivity. We all know that the more we feel appreciated, the better we perform.

❏ *Learn to listen.* Active listening, listening with sensitivity and respect, is an important part of a culture that fosters respect. Again, this is true for employees at all levels of the organization.

❏ *Provide optimism training.* What a wonderful gift to the employee and the organization alike, to teach employees to see the best in themselves, in others, in situations, and in the company.

CONCLUSION

When it comes to training, learning, and education, the role of companies in the development of the future workforce will be critical. From the basics of reading, writing, and math, through the technical and specific skills needed to perform a particular job, all the way to ethics, respect, and trust, companies, in large part, will be the ones to mold this emerging workforce.

We will need to lose the common concept that "we only train to keep." Instead, companies will be teaching employees because it's consistent with the core beliefs of the company, it's the right thing to do, and it does, in fact, pay off in the long run.

Companies will need to embrace learning as the opportunity that it is, and work to deliver learning in as many ways, in as many styles, and as many times as the future workforce will require. Both employer and employee will benefit from this endeavor.

NOTES

1. ATOFINA press release, "Local Teachers Make Noise with Hands-On Science," Philadelphia, July 2003.

2. Natalie Allen, interview, August 2003.

3. Sara Rimer, "Finding That Today's Students Are Bright, Eager and Willing to Cheat," *The New York Times*, July 2, 2003, p. B8.

4. Anna Muoio, "Cisco's Quick Study," *Fast Company*, p. 287.

5. David Finegold and Susan Mohrman, "What Do Employees Really Want? The Perception vs. the Reality." The Center for Effective Organizations, The Mar-

shall School of Business, University of Southern California. Report presented at World Economic Forum, Davos Switzerland, January 2001.

6. June Barry, interview, July 2003.

CHAPTER 10

FORMULA FOR THE FUTURE

FLEXIBILITY, RESPECT, AND TONS OF COMMUNICATION

I was an English major in college, so the importance of language and its effective use has always been a personal priority. It gave me a skill set I was able to leverage right into a career . . . as an obituary editor for a small newspaper. While I waited for people to die so that I would have work to do, I decided that I would rather help people who were living than write about them once they were dead. It is ironic to me, then, that after all the research and all the years of work experience, I have come full circle—back to my roots as an English major. Not only because I have written a book, but also because my core beliefs come back to the forefront.

How we speak to others and, perhaps more importantly, how we listen to each other are the most critical paths to success, both personally and professionally. Going into this project, I was intrigued by the future, eager to learn and to apply all that I know and have experienced, and ready to suggest the impact of the new workforce trends on human resources. The future is complex, so much is happening, and the changes will be so dramatic. I was sure that the implications must be equally complex and dramatic. Instead, however, I have found through my research on each and every one of the trends, as well as their impact on human resources, that a return to basics will have the best effect on the future of business. Open-minded flexibility, mutual respect, and clear and consistent communication will be the trilogy for success in the future.

BE FLEXIBLE

Over and over again throughout the book I have stressed the growing importance of flexibility in dealing with the workforce of the future. The emerging workforce doesn't seem nearly so scary if it is approached with an open mind and a willingness to be flexible.

Clear business goals for productivity and profit will no longer translate to rigorous, universal HR policies and procedures. Since the needs of the new workforce will be as unique as each individual worker, one solution for all will be impossible. Customized HR policies and programs will enable individuals to create a unique plan of action and performance measures that best serve both the company and the worker. This could include alternative work hours, bringing family members to work, or assistance in taking a well-prepared dinner home. Companies that embrace fair and equitable flexibility in a creative manner will win the coming war for talent.

RESPECT EVERY INDIVIDUAL IN EVERY SITUATION

Differences are to be expected, accepted, and respected. This ties in very closely with trust. Businesses will set strategies and performance measures. Then, they will need to step back and trust. A trusted and respected worker will very rarely let you down. If someone does disappoint you, take action. Respect and flexibility by no means allow for lack of performance. They relate instead to the methods and means, the time and place, for achieving performance.

Companies in the future may want to consider hiring a Legacy Officer whose job is to instill and protect the core values throughout the organization by communicating the values. This important communication will extend from new-hire orientation through work life and even to employee alumni.

COMMUNICATION IS VITAL TO FUTURE SUCCESS

Through every interview conducted, every book or article read, and every personal story heard, the resounding truth remained the same: The most successful people and the most successful companies place high priority on communications. There are books galore that describe how to communicate better. There are courses to help individuals present flawlessly or write effectively. However, the changes accompanying the emerging workforce of the future will challenge even the most adept and proficient communicator. Strategy and planning will be critical.

- ❑ *Establish the importance of communication.* Communication can't be a sometime thing and it definitely can't be a one-way street. You must make it clear that the lines of communication are open in both directions—employees will be provided information, and management will listen to their concerns and suggestions.

- ❑ *Define communication as part of company culture.* Include communication as a key component of company culture during orientation and ongoing training. Your company literature and handbook should also stress the importance of communication.

- ❑ *Make open communication part of the company mission.* State it often. In particular, place priority on communication without ramification. Employees should have no fear of reprisal if they give voice to their legitimate complaints.

- ❑ *Set up an internal communications manager.* Create a position that is part of senior management. Elevate communication into its own department. Include the director of communications on the management team.

- ❑ *Start an internal campaign.* Appoint a committee to come up with a creative communications campaign to share the mission and vision of the company.

- ❑ *Remember that listening is part of communication.* Just as there are two sides to every story, there are two sides to every communication. Listening is equally as important a component of communication as telling. Keeping employees informed is good policy, but so is listening to what they say—both positive and negative.

- ❑ *Train for communication.* Train senior management to communicate effectively, with sensitivity and respect. An important part of this training will be active and effective listening.

Employee Focus Group on Communication

Ask employees for ideas relative to communication methods and messages. Gather a diverse group of no more than twenty employees at a time, and facilitate discussion around these types of questions:

1. How do you like to hear from the company? Audio, video, e-mail, at work, at home, in person, in large groups, in small groups, or one-on-one may be only a few of the ideas they come up with. Notice differences in communication preferences among different generations, backgrounds, etc.

2. What topics do you want to hear about?

3. Who do you want to hear from?

4. Where and what time of day?

MAKING SURE YOUR MESSAGE GETS ACROSS

Establishing communication as a fundamental part of your organization's culture is an excellent starting point, but you must also find ways to get employees to listen to what you're saying. This can be done by making your communication fun and relevant and by encouraging employee involvement in the process.

❑ *Use Madison Avenue style.* At CGI, we have a saying when we are going about communicating a new benefits program for the employees of a client: We want to do it with "Madison Avenue style." This means tailoring your communications with employees as a advertising campaign, using:
  ❑ Bright colors
  ❑ Clear messages
  ❑ Clever and creative word choice
  ❑ Graphically appealing presentations

Remember that employees are used to the speed, flash, and intensity of advertising, movies, and television. If you want to convey your messages effectively, you have to get their attention. According to Tierney Communications and Blank Rome LLC, the attention level for communications has changed significantly over the past half-century, as shown in Figure 10-1.

Our job as company communicators, therefore, will be to headline with rapid speed our message to get attention, but then to follow up with details, clarity, repetition, and interesting points.

❑ *Use testimonials of clients and employees.* One of the most effective ways to bring home a message is to show endorsement by third parties. Companies can share letters from clients, or share employee stories of why the company is a good place to work.

❑ *Invite questions and answers.* Whether in an open forum or employee chat room, encourage employee and customer input and questions. Direct inquiries and comments to the proper department head. Place time guidelines for responses, and share answers with everyone, not just with the one who asked the questions. Train the responders to answer questions well and to the point.

Figure 10-1. Change in length of time of sound bites.

1948	75 seconds
1968	60 seconds
1988	45 seconds
1995	20 seconds
2000	15 seconds
2004	10 seconds or less

COMMUNICATING WITH A DECENTRALIZED WORKFORCE

Employees in the future will be working at all different hours and in many different locations. This will call for ongoing communications in many forms.

❑ *E-Mail, IM, and Text-Messaging.* Quick updates on company news or crisis information that will be in the mass media before management can speak directly to employees are examples of the types of messages that can be easily and quickly shared with employees who are not all working at the same location.

❏ *Video Conferencing.* Video conferencing will increasingly allow employees at different locations to have "face-to-face" meetings or training without the downtime and expense of travel.

❏ *Virtual Staff Meetings.* Private Web casts, conference calls, or password-protected chat rooms can replace the traditional weekly meeting in the conference room.

❏ *Daily E-Newsletter.* Employees can get a daily dose of news and events from the company. You also may want to encourage employees to contribute to the newsletter.

❏ *Home Page.* Companies can create a custom home page for employee computers that updates what's new and offers links to key sources of information that employees need on benefits, job openings, etc.

COMMUNICATION AND THE FIVE TRENDS

Your company's relationship with the new workforce will depend on how you communicate with your employees. From day-to-day interaction to presenting new HR policies, everything starts with communication. Here are some quick thoughts relating communication to the five trends:

COMMUNICATION AS IT RELATES TO LONGEVITY

❏ *Use louder volume/larger print.* I know I keep repeating it, but this is an important consideration. If all it takes to get the message across to your older workers is a little tinkering with the medium, it's well worth the effort.

❏ *Use high-touch not high-tech.* Remember that for older employees, work has tremendous social ties. High-touch is highly preferred to high-tech. It's not that they can't use or understand technology; it's that the personal interaction is very important to them.

❏ *Reinforce communications in person.* Whenever possible, send a person from the communications team to talk directly to the workers.

All employees will like this approach, but older workers especially appreciate the direct communication.

❏ *Meet them where they are.* Companies can convey or reinforce messages in the lunchroom or on the shuttle bus. Bringing the message to employees enhances the effect.

COMMUNICATION AS IT RELATES TO MULTIPLE HOUSEHOLD TYPES

❏ *Let employees determine where to receive company mail.* Whether driven by privacy issues or a complex home life, employees can decide the best way to receive company news and information. It can come to their home, office, or even a P.O. box.

❏ *Offer communications training for family issues.* The concept here is not one of providing a counselor/arbitrator who gets involved in issues. Instead, companies can host communication and listening skills workshops on different topics such as:
  ❏ Getting past "no" with toddlers
  ❏ Getting in touch with teenagers
  ❏ Keeping respect in communicating with elders
  ❏ Explaining how multiple generations can live well together
  ❏ Explaining unique home situations

COMMUNICATION AS IT RELATES TO THE GENERATIONS

Communicating across the generations will pose its own challenges.

❏ *Jargon Workshops.* Words take on different meanings to different generations. Take, for example, my young friend telling me that being "fat," spelled "phat," is a good thing, as is being "the bomb," an even harder transition given that I was hiding under my desk from "bombs" in grade school. Divergent meanings across culture and heritage also are common. In response, companies can offer workshops on jargon and new words that are becoming common.

❏ *Online Word Wizard.* Through the Web site or home page, companies can offer a link that offers clarity to the confused about words and their meanings. This hybrid dictionary can provide explanations of new words, jargon, old expressions, and archaic terms, thus being a helpful tool to all generations.

❑ *E-Mail Etiquette.* HOW AM I SUPPOSED TO KNOW THAT TYPING ALL IN CAPITALS MEANS I'M SHOUTING? E-mail etiquette, abbreviations, expressions, and implied meanings abound. Companies can offer helpful tips and guidelines to employees about these and other high-tech issues.

❑ *Human Communications Etiquette.* At the same time, the younger generations in particular may benefit from tips and guidelines for communicating face-to-face. For example, the finest surgeons of the future may come from the youngest in our population, the generation I called the Millennials. They will be among the first to be trained extensively on the use of robotic medical technology. These are predicted to be mostly young males who have spent countless hours on computers, playing computer games, IM'ing their friends instead of calling on the phone. As such, they will join organizations as highly trained, highly skilled technicians, but they may have had little opportunity to develop their communication skills. These technically proficient young doctors may need communications and sensitivity training. This same perspective will be needed for all the IT wizards who join your company and may need communications coaching.

COMMUNICATION AS IT RELATES TO DIVERSITY

❑ *Communication Through Various Methods.* Companies need to be sensitive to differing communications needs of individuals both inside and outside of their organization. Consider publishing internal and external communication through various means such as:
  ❑ Auditory or Braille for the blind
  ❑ Printed in a format for the visually impaired
  ❑ Video/audio for those who are illiterate

❑ *Translation into Various Languages.* Translating into languages other than English is not a new idea. However, companies will find the need for translation more pervasive than ever before.

❏ *Communications Watchdog Team.* Establish a group of employees from diverse backgrounds who check for offensive material included in company advertising, brochures, printed material, and employee communications. Not just politically correct, but also accurately stated.

COMMUNICATION AS IT RELATES TO TRUST, RESPECT, AND ETHICS

❏ *Talk without fear.* As I consider all these suggestions for placing corporate priority on open communication, one important point keeps coming to mind: Absolutely, positively key to open company communications is that employees must feel able to share without fear of retribution. A key to building trust and respect into the culture of any organization is that employees know that they can speak freely and know that what they say will be heard, respected, and considered. They should not feel afraid to make waves. They can't feel that they will be punished or even fired for speaking up.

❏ *"Blab it all out."* Companies can put together meetings of a cross-section of employees where they are encouraged and rewarded to "blab it all out." Tell-all does not mean all negative, however. Sharing ideas for new ways to do things that may seem outlandish or sticking up for one's individual interests are included. Telling even the smallest, most mundane reasons that a company or an individual is appreciated are included, too.

❏ *Set up a communication corner.* Companies can run a monthly article in the company newsletter or e-zine that gives an example of workplace communication that worked effectively. Examples include an employee suggestion that was accepted and implemented, an effective client communication, or a mistake that was learned from.

Do the Right Thing

I have a friend who is president of concrete company. One time, a huge barrier was pushed by a heavy gust of wind, crushing and killing a client worker at the job site. My friend's company had made the concrete barrier, but had no legal responsibility in the accident. His corporate lawyers advised him to do nothing, in fear that it would seem like an admission of guilt. Then he talked to the CEO, who told him to do what he thought was right.

He felt it was right that he do something. So he paid for the funeral and started a foundation to pay college tuition for the worker's children. He communicated his deepest sympathy openly to both the other company and the family of the worker. He also shared the story with his own company. In short, he did the ethically right thing and communicated about it openly. Bottom line, there were no negative ramifications.

DON'T FORGET THE PERSONAL TOUCH

As we've noted, there are times when high-tech communication enables companies to get messages to all their employees quickly and easily. However, sometimes high-tech forms of communication can actually detract from the message, damage its intent, and even offend people. Time and energy should be devoted not only to the proper context and word choice for a message, but also to the best and most appropriate medium by which to deliver that message.

Consideration must be given to the best medium for all communication, not just the big news or the bad news. For example, I know of one company that was considering adding disability coverage to its employee benefits. Many of the employees of this company were young and they had no idea what disability insurance was or why they might need it. So they would have to be convinced that young people do become disabled.

To communicate the message about disability insurance, a simple e-mail was sent to all employees stating that the company was considering adding disability insurance for employees; the cost would be x; and if you were interested in having this insurance, please reply by next Friday.

Not surprisingly, the coverage wasn't elected. There was no explanation of what disability insurance covers and why it can be important. It was only described as a cost; no benefits were described. Presentations about the coverage, sales pitches even, would have made an important difference. At a minimum, more information should have been provided about what disability insurance covers, and when and why it's necessary.

Here are a few ways to add the personal touch to company communications:

- ❏ *Leverage mentors.* Use mentors to spread messages and gather feedback about messages in a more intimate way.

- ❏ *Encourage "best friends."* CGI instituted a "Best Friends" program many years ago. It was intended to ensure that the culture was conveyed each time a new team member was hired. Some of the best friends initiated by the program are still together decades later, having supported each other through personal and work-related triumphs and tragedies.

- ❏ *Get management out there walking around.* Whenever possible, insist that managers deliver messages and ask questions in person. Avoid relying on e-mail and instant messaging for everything. Employees often are much more at ease when talking to managers at their own work stations.

- ❏ *Use a roving communications manager.* Companies can keep the high-touch in high-tech by employing a human messenger who actually visits employees on a regular basis and keeps the culture of an organization alive while communicating messages as well as repeating core values. This is particularly important for those working at home. When my daughter was in nursery school, her teacher made it a point to visit each child's home, visit her bedroom, and have a chat. Imagine a communications manager rotating visits to see the work location, chat, and share company news.

Don't Hide Behind Technology

Sitting in the office of an employee one day, we were meeting about a client concern that needed immediate attention. About 6:00 P.M., we took a break, and my coworker typed a message into her computer and hit send. Almost immediately, there was a quick ding indicating a response. She typed and sent again. Another ding. Type. Ding. Type. Ding. What was going on?

It turns out that she was "communicating" with her husband, who also works for CGI and was sitting just a few feet away, down the hall. They were arguing electronically about who should go pick up the kids. Call me old-fashioned, but I still prefer to talk to people face to face, even when arguing.

The point is not to hide behind technology. We need to figure out the best way to communicate. In many ways, technology greatly enhances our ability to connect globally and instantly. However, it also can be a barrier to interpersonal communication that is so vital to our human spirit.

MAKE COMMUNICATION OPEN AND ACCEPTING

The new workforce will be an eye-opening challenge, with each employee bringing his or her own unique perspective to the table. This workforce will necessitate a culture of openness and acceptance so that communication can flow freely in all directions. This won't happen by itself. Many companies think they have an open communication culture, but that's just because they say they do—they don't truly welcome and communicate challenges. I know of one CEO in particular who perceives that employees are encouraged to share their opinions, ideas, and views. In reality, however, most of her employees would say that her credo is "Everyone is entitled to my opinion."

Attending a lecture recently, I heard the head of a major cable company describe a competitor that had a culture where all meetings were required to be upbeat and wonderful. News was always delivered in a cheerleading style. The company dealt with problems behind closed doors or not at all. Employees were kept in the dark. That company was slipping in productivity and was eventually acquired.

The acquiring company has a very different culture where challenges are embraced, discussed, probed, dissected, and solved. Both good and bad news are shared. This new company is thriving. The lesson? Communication must be true and open—good and bad alike need to be shared.

HOW TO EFFECTIVELY DELIVER YOUR MESSAGES

Getting your messages across and understood is crucial to good communications. Here are some basic guidelines you can use that will increase the probability that your messages will be received:

❏ *Clarity.* At all levels of an organization, from the management team through all employees, any message must be as clear and simple as possible.

❏ *Reinforcement.* It is a basic concept that bears repeating: Effective communication requires repetition. For the most important messages, once and done will not do. Repetition can come in many ways:

    ❏ *Annual Updates.* It is fairly common for companies to have annual meetings that review financials, especially with shareholders. Expand that concept to cover other key messages of the organization. For example, a company can annually:

        Highlight promotions.

        Announce employee awards.

        Celebrate employee anniversaries.

        Have the morale committee give an update.

        Ask the employee judiciary committee to share key findings or resolutions.

    ❏ *Ongoing Column/Feature.* A regular communication such as an employee newsletter can have an ongoing column that addresses a certain topic or reinforces a certain value. Open communication, for example, can be reinforced by a monthly "Ask the CEO" column, where employee letters are published along with the executive's response.

    ❏ *Multiple Mediums.* When new messages are introduced, a very effective way to ensure that diverse employees understand the message is by repeating it through several mediums. A member of management may deliver the message verbally, reinforced by a Power Point presentation. Handouts can repeat the message and be on the employees' desks the next day. Newsletters or blast e-mails can highlight and repeat the key messages over a series of weeks.

    ❏ *Multiple Sources.* Messages can be effectively reinforced by having employees hear them consistently from many sources. For example, a new employee may hear about certain policies and procedures during orientation, then again from the CEO of the company, then from a supervisor who is asked a question, and finally from peer employees who sit on the employee judiciary committee.

❑ *External Reinforcement.* Some messages can be reinforced when employees see or hear them through the company's advertising to external audiences. When a company supports nonprofits and charities or undertakes community outreach, it shows employees that certain ethics and values aren't just in speeches and articles, they are in the very fiber of the company and its leaders.

Myles Martel is a prominent communication and leadership consultant to executives throughout the world. He cites the following points as critical for communication in the future:

❑ *Multistep Approach.* A single communication for delivering a tough message to a large or broad audience is not likely to be effective. A campaign or multistep approach using several mediums (e.g., Internet, private meetings, letters) is usually necessary for ensuring that such messages have the desired reach and resonance.

❑ *Questions and Answers.* The interactive piece of communication is steadily becoming as important, if not more important, than the presentation. Taking employees' questions is critical to developing authentic workplace communication, because the answers are regarded as more credible than "prespun" presentations. Therefore, try to anticipate the more challenging questions and craft responses that satisfy the questioner and target audience while supporting your communication goals. As such, training presenters in the skill of answering questions effectively will be an important aspect of future training in presentation skills.[1]

EXTERNAL COMMUNICATIONS

While the majority of the ideas and discussion in this chapter focus on communication within an organization, here are a couple of key points relative to *external* communications.

❑ *Be consistent.* Whether written, spoken, or implied, communication must be consistent. Internal messages must be consistent with external messages. Advertising must reinforce company culture. Multiple media and multiple sources must be coordinated to convey the same message as well as the same flavor.

❏ *Be believable.* Communication to the outside world must be believable. Claims for service, delivery, or product should not be exaggerated.

❏ *Consider sharing resources.* Companies that are not afraid to communicate in an open dialogue with other companies—and even competitors—can benefit greatly from shared resource solutions. Here are a couple of examples.

STORY 1: A TALE OF TWO CLIENTS

We have one client that had a large workforce of drivers that delivered propane throughout the winter. In the summer, these drivers didn't have much to do. We have another client that had little use for their drivers in the winter, due to road conditions, but used them often during the summer. Opportunity knocked. We facilitated a dialogue between the two clients to investigate the possibility of a shared workforce of drivers. To carry this off, however, communicators to the drivers needed expert skills to help in new thinking. This required creative, clear communications to share company culture, style, mission, and the vision of these two companies.

STORY 2: LET THERE BE PARKING

In Florida, a church and a synagogue were able to communicate effectively and negotiate the shared purchase of the land between their two facilities to use for additional parking. This arrangement has worked very well because the Sabbath, holidays, and high holy days of each congregation do not overlap. In fact, the two groups have also begun to trade baby-sitting for high holidays.

CONCLUSION

For individuals and for companies, communication will be the key that separates old thinking from new thinking. As think tanks and task forces set out to prepare their organizations for the future, careful attention must be given to how communication will happen. Effective communication within our organizations and to the outside world will enable companies to make a difference and succeed.

I look forward to a time when each person is judged by their own unique skills and contribution, regardless of any other factor—age, gender, family setting, heritage, or faith. What we share will be most important—mutual respect and core values. The company that embraces and welcomes all of these differences and similarities will attract the best talent to work in its organization and enjoy the best mechanisms of keeping employees. Success and profitability will most certainly follow. The challenge is to start planning for the new workforce now. Shout your successes, applaud your failures, and get known as the company that is ready for the future.

NOTE

1. Myles Martel, interview, September 2003.

FUTURE THINK TANK

CONDUCTING A SURVEY OF YOUR EMPLOYEES TO GET READY FOR THE NEW WORKFORCE

With so many fresh ideas, companies may struggle with how to start working with this new workforce.

Throughout the book, I suggested using small focus group meetings with suggested questions, easy thought provokers. Now I suggest that you gather all of your company ideas and make it rewarding for you and your fellow employees by conducting a more comprehensive survey. By working on this you'll be able to use this internal data to start getting ready for the future. In addition, you will create a positive and energized group of internal employees to start spreading the word about how your company cares and is getting ready for the future.

FIRST STEPS

1. Establish a focus group (or two, three, or more depending on the size of your company).

2. Involve someone who represents each of the first four emerging trends.

   Longevity: Elderly workers, if you have some
   Household Types: Representatives of varied household types
   Generations: All age brackets

> *Diversity*: Different races, religions, genders, and handicapped employees

Although you cannot select representatives for Trend 5—*Trust, Respect, and Ethics*—we have included questions for this topic.

3. Reward participants, with foods, status, time off, etc.

4. Ask for a commitment of six two-hour sessions, perhaps starting early, staying late, or over lunch.

5. Have the best facilitator you can find within your company, or hire someone from outside your company. E-mail or call us if you need help finding the right facilitator.

6. Have a comfortable room with a flipchart and markers for recording the ideas from the session.

7. Make it fun and exciting. If you stir up controversy, get even more excited. Remember—the point is to gather data from your own workforce on how to get ready for the new workforce.

SESSION ONE

HUMAN RESOURCE POLICY

1. Rank the following time-off policies in order of importance to you.
   a. Vacation time
   b. Company holidays
   c. Personal days
   d. Flexible time
   e. Varied work schedule
   f. Training time
   g. Academic study
   h. Giving back to the community
   i. Sabbatical
   j. Exercise time
   k. Other _____

2. Rank the importance of the following:
   a. Ethical company

    b. Profitable company

    c. Company that supports work/life balance issues

    d. Company that is strong on career pathing

    e. Company that supplies all the latest tools for work

    f. Other _____

3. Pick the top three of the following possible additional services, in order of priority:

    a. Concierge services (car repair service, dry cleaning drop-off)

    b. Hot meals to go at the end of the day

    c. Shuttle bus service

    d. Advocate provided for help with medical issues

    e. Investment advice

    f. Financial planning

    g. Work/life planning

    h. Elder/child care

    i. On-site gym

    j. Other _____

4. List open-ended suggestions regarding company guidelines on the following:

    a. Lateness

    b. Absenteeism

    c. Discipline

    d. Harassment

    e. Complaint resolution

    f. Presenteeism

    g. Underachievement

5. List open-ended suggestions for what would make the company a better, easier place in which to work:

SESSION TWO

RECRUITING

1. Rank by order of importance the way you would look for a new job:
   a. Friend or relative recommendation
   b. Internet, want ads
   c. Newspaper want ads
   d. Positive press about the company
   e. Listing on Internet data base
   f. Headhunter or search firm
   g. Other _____

2. Rank the information you want to know about the company before you join, in order of importance:
   a. Compensation policy
   b. Benefits
   c. Company vision
   d. Coworkers
   e. Boss
   f. HR policies
   g. Career path
   h. Training and development opportunities
   i. Culture
   j. Other _____

3. Rank how you would like to hear about the company, in order of importance:
   a. In person from inside recruiter
   b. In person from outside recruiter
   c. From direct supervisor
   d. From brochure for applicants
   e. Directly from someone working in the company
   f. From Web site
   g. Other _____

4. Open-ended suggestions regarding recruiting and attracting the best candidates (how, where, when, who, etc.):

5. Open-ended suggestions for creating the best talent pool:

SESSION THREE

COMPENSATION AND BENEFITS

1. Rank in order of importance the following:
   a. Base pay
   b. Incentive pay
   c. Stock options
   d. Medical coverage
   e. Retirement plan
   f. Time off
   g. Retiree health care
   h. Other _____

2. Rank in order of importance the following:
   a. Disability insurance
   b. Life insurance
   c. Employee Assistance Program
   d. Rx insurance
   e. Dental insurance
   f. Long-term care
   g. Vision care
   h. Wellness benefits
   i. Other _____

3. Pick the top three of the following possible additional benefits, in order of priority:
   a. More company money to health-care premium
   b. More company money to retirement plan

    c. More company money to retiree health care

    d. More disability coverage

    e. Company money to automobile insurance

    f. More vacation time

    g. More holidays

    h. More sick time

    i. More training time

    j. More discretionary time

    k. Other _____

4. Open-ended discussion on new compensation ideas for the future:

5. Open-ended discussion on new benefit ideas for the future:

SESSION FOUR

TRAINING AND LEARNING

1. Rank in order of importance to you:
   a. On-the-job training
   b. Computer skills training
   c. Supervisory/management training
   d. Basic business skills
      i. How to read a financial report
      ii. How to write a business memo
   e. Career development
   f. Other _____

2. Rank the way you best learn:
   a. Interesting teacher lecture
   b. Questions and answers from a manual, audiotape, or video
   c. Reading (on your own) a procedure manual with written instructions
   d. One-on-one with someone showing you (coaching)
   e. E-training
   f. Other _____

3. Rank your best time and place to learn:
   a. At home with materials
   b. At the office, during the work day
   c. At the office, during lunch
   d. After work
   e. Before work
   f. In the computer lab at work
4. Open-ended suggestions for additional training desired, such as:
   a. Time management
   b. Parenting skills
   c. Life planning
   d. Wellness sessions
   e. Other _____
5. Open-ended discussion on how each of the trends affects learning, and suggestions for courses and materials tied to the five trends:

SESSION FIVE

COMMUNICATION

This final session should be a wrap-up of all preceding work. The open-ended question for this session is: "What are all the many ways we should and could communicate with each other?" Brainstorm and share as many fresh ideas as possible.

INDEX

About the Author

Harriet Hankin is the president and an owner of CGI Consulting Group, Inc., a benefits design, consulting, and administration company. Since joining CGI in 1985, she has been instrumental in helping grow the company from a dozen employees to being a recognized leader in unique and creative benefit solutions. Prior to joining CGI, Harriet was director of corporate benefits for Aramark, a worldwide, diversified management company, and manager of compensation and benefits for Provident National Bank.

Harriet was named one of Pennsylvania's Best 50 Women in Business for 2000; one of 25 Women of Distinction for 2000; a winner of the Ernst and Young Entrepreneur of the Year Award for 2001; and 2001 Businesswoman of the Year by the Great Valley Regional Chamber of Commerce.

Ms. Hankin can be reached at hhankin@cgiconsulting.com.